We Side with
the Morning

Here is a book of an entire year of daily prayers that are door openers to silence and reflection. Cleary's use of new names for God creatively make them in themselves two-word prayers, as in, "O God of the have-nots and the voiceless." His prayers courageously wrestle with darkness, religious confusion, and God's inexplicable ways. His excellent introduction on how to pray is itself worth the price of this book.

Ed Hays
Author of *Prayers for a Planetary Pilgrim*

Cleary's calendar of prayers is for those who want to start praying in a new key. It will appeal to seekers and skeptics, and to those for whom the institutional church has not felt like a welcoming home, but who continue to yearn for a language with which to name the Divine. His suggestions on how to pray and his insights into the life of prayer are accessible, useful, intimate, and moving. Do not skip the introduction!

Jane Redmont
Author of *When in Doubt, Sing*

We Side with the Morning

Daily Prayers to the God of Hope

William Cleary

Author of *How the Wild Things Pray*

SORIN BOOKS Notre Dame, Indiana

© 2009 by Ave Maria Press, Inc.

All rights reserved. No part of this book may be used or reproduced in any manner whatsoever, except in the case of reprints in the context of reviews, without written permission from Sorin Books®, P.O. Box 428, Notre Dame, IN 46556.

www.sorinbooks.com

ISBN-10 1-933495-19-7   ISBN-13 978-1-933495-19-4

Cover and text design by David Scholtes.

Cover image © Jiunlimited.com

Printed and bound in the United States of America.

Library of Congress Cataloging-in-Publication Data
Cleary, William.
  We side with the morning : daily prayers to the God of hope / William Cleary.
    p. cm.
  Includes index.
ISBN 978-1-933495-19-4 (pbk.)
1. Prayers. 2. Devotional calendars. I. Title.
  BL560.C545 2009
  242'.8--dc22

                                                          2009015148

INTRODUCTION

An Introduction: Learning to Pray

Prayer is talking to God. My mother whispered to me one night as she tucked me into bed, "Say your prayers, Billy, as if you meant every word." I have tried to do that ever since, but over the years it has become complicated. Instead of "Our Father," I want to say "Our Father and Mother." That's become commonplace these days, even in public prayers. Other new forms of address are common too, naming God "Holy Mystery of Life" or "Loving Energy" or in theologian Elizabeth Johnson's words, "Relational Liveliness that Energizes the Universe!"

I put together these 365 prayers day by day over a year's time. I wrote them often in the darkness of an early hour, and in the shadowland of doubt and mystification, as is obvious in the text. They appeared on a fragile Web site where spiritual seekers came browsing, and hopefully, these prayer-words guided people to places they had never been before: to shadowland, to baffle-land, and even to disbelief-land. The gyroscope of honesty always causes trouble to flight plans of prayer. Meditation and prayer time that is honest can be disconcerting to those who are very used to conventional travel.

In learning to pray, it's wonderful to try to follow the guidance of the fourth Century mystic, St. Denis: "The truly divine knowledge of God is that which is known by unknowing." His comment was remembered throughout the early history of Christian mysticism, and was famously quoted in an anonymous classic called "The Cloud of Unknowing," a fourteenth century work which may well have been anonymous because the author was feminine. It sounds that way to me.

Unknowing is a mysterious concept, but at a minimum it suggests that, in seeking "a truly divine knowledge of God," we approach the loving energy at the heart of reality, God, with both humility and intimacy—with readiness for doubt and darkness along with faith. That is the style of these prayers—which are only peripherally and metaphorically in the tradition of The Cloud of Unknowing itself. The metaphor of a cloud helps us deal with the same doubts and darkness experienced by Mother Teresa which only came to light in 2006 when the Church was first exploring the possibility of canonizing her as a saint. She says in private letters—in the book *Mother Teresa: Come Be My Light* (2007)— "inside it is all dark and feeling that I am cut off from God." We could hypothesize that she was experiencing a kind of cloud of unknowing, something many an ordinary human—unheroic, regular folks—has to put up with too.

"Hallowed be thy name" is a prayer I have said since my bedtime prayers of childhood. When you really hallow something or someone's name, you start with silence: a minute of silence perhaps. It is the only fitting action to take at the start of a reflective time. Sometimes only silence is satisfying. When recalling a great tragedy like September 11, we often take a full minute for silence. Or when recalling a great wonder, perhaps silence would be best too—thinking about creation itself comes to mind. Instead of filling up the air immediately with a Gregorian chant Te Deum, or hymns singing "Thanks be to God," we might just say nothing at all and let the awesomeness sink in.

In fact, maybe our silence in this case would last "from now on": Never again uttering the words "God" or "Yahweh," just say nothing and hallow the thought. That's the Jewish way, for instance. In fact, that may be exactly what Jesus of Nazareth was referring to in his "Our Father's" opening phrase: "Hallowed be thy name." Thus, for some at least, saying nothing about God, or the mystery of God, and just observing it all with awe, could be our prayer.

Maybe you are a person who says you cannot pray at all. If so, my hope is that these prayers can lead you to silence. And then what? As hard as it may be to believe, prayer can be as much a part of your life as breathing. You may doubt if you can ever find words to say to God, or to the Vast Silence of creation, or will never find a way to speak back your own words to the utterances of God heard among beautiful created things. Try this, especially when faced with great beauty: *simply put your hand on your heart.*

Is this not a kind of natural gesture of gratitude? Does it not express an attitude of hallowed silence, of humble appreciation? Most people would see it as such: your hand or both hands on your heart speaks volumes to those who observe it. And if there is a God, God observes it. You have prayed. Use it daily and hourly if you like. For me it never wears out. Sometimes it "says it all," all I can manage to say and all I want to say. On my deathbed—if I am conscious—I hope I have the energy to put my hand on my heart.

In a way, I can turn all this upside-down and admit that I am philosophically against most spoken prayer. The more you think about our world, the more silent and over-awed you become. Both the physics and the metaphysics of our surroundings are baffling. The speed of light is beyond belief, unbelievable in a way: six times around the world in one second? No one can think that thought! It's too fast! Something sweeping around the earth six times in one second? You must simply take it on faith, even if you can't imagine it.

Maybe too our instinctual prayers to God are patently foolish and childish: if God is infinitely compassionate and all-knowing, then nothing we could say will improve things. Obviously we can't pinch God—as much as we might like to. Then there is the mystery of creation's order: if lions and dinosaurs and all animals are the fashioning of a merciful creator, then why do they all have to live by eating each other, frequently alive? I must admit that I am baffled by that—aren't you? And bafflement makes you silent, not prayerful. *Unless* your words of prayer lead you toward that silence! And unless it is your silence that should properly be considered your "prayer."

Some people tell me they have given up on prayer. Why? It doesn't work, and it doesn't work for them. And it's all too impossible to figure out: it doesn't make sense. Perhaps, in a way, such folks are the wisest. On the other hand, I think it makes sense to pray as long as we realize that talking to God is like talking to your dog. We speak in English to our dog, but he mostly pays attention to our smell. Similarly, we may soar around in the cloud of unknowing trying to talk to God, but God of course is mostly paying attention for the aroma of compassion for those who are lonely and in need, those who are thirsty and hungry, and whom we help with water, food, and housing.

In my local church, there is actually a member who says he doesn't believe in God, yet he comes to church, and he is the first one to donate to deserving causes, the most quick to come to the aid of anyone in need; he brought up a homeless and marginalized child right along with his own family. It is almost humorous to hear him say he is an atheist while he thinks believers are themselves funny.

The best prayers, of course, are those we find within us and utter in the depths of our hearts, and which may come forth whether we want them to or not. The words of this book are the prayers I found in my own heart that way. You are welcome to all the "unknowing" that is in them. They reflect a world vision that is less profound than humble, partly ridiculous, and human: the best I can do. May they find echoes in your own heart as well.

William Cleary

JANUARY

January 1

We Hear Your Whisper: For an alert piety

We hear your whisper, Silent Creator, in the scent of
moonflowers closing their blooms as the sun rises. Your being
glows there, and everywhere that life is, sometimes stopping
us in our tracks to pause and sense the sweet bouquet of a
living thing thriving out of sight, but much in evidence to the
alert. Give us ears to hear your messages in the air around us,
irrepressible Spirit, alert to the soaring music just below the
surface of life.
Amen.

January 2

You Answer: In touch with God

Ultimate Mystery, Holy God, womb and creator of all that is,
you hear the cries of our being whenever our hearts beat. You
hear the body language of our needs and desires in our every
motion and action. Your answer to our communication is the
continuance of our being, the energies of our living organs,
and the magnetic pull of our destiny. It is an elegant two-way
interaction, and we rejoice enthusiastically to be part of it and
aware of it.
Amen.

January 3

Living Energy: Appreciating life itself

Living Energy, who knows us the way you created us as well
as the way we have shaped ourselves, we greet you in the
Cloud of Unknowing, reaching for mutuality with you, some
level of real communication. Along with you we agonize for
the earthly failures of love, and for human pain and violence,
and with you we rejoice at the slanting morning sunrise and
the heroism sprouting like the wildflowers surprising us
everywhere. We give thanks for the best parts of earthly life
and long to enhance it however we can today.

Amen.

January 4

Your Generosity: Finding God in the morning

Your immeasurable generosity, O Holy Mystery, fills us
with awe whenever we are mindful of it: as our earth spins
gigantically toward the morning sun, as uncountable leaves
reach out to take in the lovely wild rain, as living bodies
awaken, whisper courage to loved ones, and the music of
human life sparks to life. Darker realities awaken too, but
we side with the morning, with the urgent sun, with life
Immeasurable. God of life, be near today.

Amen.

January 5

We Sense Your Presence: Believing in God's graciousness

One God, ultimate in intelligence and infinite in generosity and goodness, while we do not begin to understand the reality you have created in us and around us, we instinctually sense your presence in the world and especially in the mystery of personal magnetism and attractiveness, in the pleasures of friend-making and love-making, in the wonders of fertility and childbirth, in the joys of family and community. We are grateful to participate, and we listen in the music of what exists for your voice and guidance.

Amen.

January 6

Be With Us: Putting faith in God

God of comfort and encouragement, be with us in times of tragedy and disappointment, in depression and sorrow. You are the all-creative love that invented the sweet dynamism of caringness on this earth, what some Africans name *Ubuntu*, the feeling, communal heart. The challenges of human life assault us on every side, still we have you to turn to. Into your hands we surrender our hearts, for we have chosen to believe that ultimately this world of yours is benevolent, and you are ever with us despite all appearances.

Amen.

January 7

Unimaginable God: Reaching out in the darkness

Holy Unimaginable God, we sometimes find it almost
impossible to believe in you. So much in our world speaks out
against your existence: injustice and human evil most of all,
but also disease and sorrow, failure and pain. Almost any kind
of a God we can imagine would never allow the worldwide
abuse of women and children, of the poor and vulnerable. You
are a God beyond imagining, almost beyond belief. Hear our
voices. Are you there? We reach out to you in the silence and
darkness.
Amen.

January 8

Spirit Strangely Illusive: Finding God on all sides

Knowing-us God, Spirit strangely illusive but discernable
in what you have made, especially in things that are alive:
we give thanks for the pleasures of human company, for the
excitement of feeling creative and communicative, for the joys
of our life—alongside its bewildering tragedies. Give us the
inspiration we need to live life fully today, finding evidence
of your mystery and intelligence in all that is, grateful for our
part in it.
Amen.

January 9

We Dare to Name You: When yearning for justice

O God, loving parent and champion of all the oppressed,
of the have-nots, and of the voiceless—we dare to name
you thus because prophets everywhere call you a "God
of justice," a sublime name that celebrates the best in
human hearts of which you have ever been the gracious
inspiration. Share with us your spirit of compassion and
fairness, your holy quality of justice which you wish
for your world. We would be your servants and your
collaborators this day.
Amen.

January 10

God Beyond Names: Communicating with God's heart

Holy God beyond names, evident only through your creation,
the thought of you restores our hearts. We find wisdom
evident in the amazing good order of the cosmos, in the
astonishing complexities of the micro-cosmos, in the wonders
of life, of vision, of intelligence, and especially of human love.
We give reverence to the creator of these miracles of our world.
As your progeny, we desire some small measure of the same
wisdom in living our lives and dealing with the mysteries of
good and evil that challenge us.
Amen.

January 11

We Have No Certainty: Relying on the divine graciousness

Much about this life you have given us, Creating Spirit, is difficult. We have no certainty that our daily choices are the best they could be. Our connections to those we love are tenuous and weak. Our health is always ambiguous, and our community connections are unpredictable. Still we rejoice to be alive one more day, and hope for a feeling that we've done our best when day is done—with an abundance of your forgiveness when we need it. We give thanks to have your inspiring presence at today's every moment.
Amen.

January 12

All Shall Be Well: Trusting God ultimately

We know, Spirit Mystery, that something creative is happening in our lives all the time, something good going forward despite all we worry about. If even our worst fears came true, in your vast resources of artistry and invention they would be some ultimate splendor. All shall be well: that is certainly your decree and you can make it, for you are God. Out of the greatest horrors you can bring, perhaps not every dream, but every kind of ultimate and glorious consummation. May it be so.
Amen.

January 13

Thank You For Life: Blessing God as best you can

O Holy Force, Single Mind, Mystery Creator and Ever-Present
God, ocean of mystery and magnetism, enigmatic one beyond
our comprehension, we greet you this new day, this new
turning of our planet home, this new encounter with our day-
star the sun. Thank you for life another day. Thank you for
faith, for the infinitesimal knowledge of you we have. You
are our parent, and to you we turn for meaning. Our milieu is
almost too wonderful to exist: it is hard to believe—but here it
is before us. Blest are we because of you.
Amen.

January 14

We Feel You There: Knowing God awaits us

The warming sun overhead hums a heartening melody, and
all the flowers hear her voice and move to the beats and beams
of life-giving music. We feel you there, sun-like Creator, far
above us but stretching down to be within us too. When life is
over we suspect you will scoop us up totally into the vitality
of your rhythmic symphony. Some life sounds are tragic, we
know, but we feel it all has an ultimate harmony and meaning,
and we surrender to its promising mystery.
Amen.

January 15

We Are Magical: Reverencing our own being

Could we humans be more magical, more wondrous, Creator
Spirit? Well, yes: were we, for instance, without our destiny
of death. Had we, generally speaking, more bountiful hearts,
more patient, more compassionate souls—we'd be even more
magical. Still we are grateful for what wonders there are
within us, and pleased to be your companion in creation and
creativity. We honor you when we live fully, learning how to
draw love into everything, to live heart-centered lives—with a
heart for others, for ourselves, and for our earthen home.
Amen.

January 16

Your World Is Beautiful: Honoring the Creative Spirit

Mysterious Creative Spirit, designing living cells so
astonishingly complex that no computer can even
comprehensively record their microscopic wizardry: our
world, your world, is beautiful and elegant beyond words.
We give thanks. And we will attempt to live with generous
thankfulness appropriate to your own bounty. We rejoice to
know your invisible presence and surrender in reverence to
life as it is, full of mystery and promise.
Amen.

January 17

How We Know You: Trying to understand God

Massive Mystery, do we hypothesize you out of whole cloth? That we would do were we to imagine you a silver sphere at the center of the cosmos or, say, a great Warlord. Cultures have imagined you thus and have gone wrong. However, to say there exists a God of wisdom whose intellectual prowess is discoverable in the elegant design of things, say, of the human brain—this is plausible, and commonplace. A God who even hears one's voice: that's plausible too. Hold me in this faith today, Divine Enigma, my God.
Amen.

January 18

Sympathizing Spirit: Surrendering to reality

Is the sadness that sometimes occupies my heart, Holy One, perhaps a mirror-image of your own, you the sympathizing parent of us all, grieving at every tragedy in this world, however much your larger vision may give it some kind of clarifying meaning? We are not alone in our sorrow: that is comforting. Nor are you in yours. Whatever absurdity has come to pass must, in some perspective, some final and all-inclusive vision, arrive at a place of meaning and resolution far beyond our comprehension as it may be. Could this be true? It is our hope.
Amen.

January 19

Your Incarnate Self: Finding God in creation

Holy Mystery, who has necessarily incarnated your own self
in your creations, eluding us until we break the code and
decipher your messages and promises in all that is, we hear
your voice with reverence. We seek the comfort of your artistry
in those we love and those who love us, and in the history of
time and the extravagance of evolution, in our heart's own
deepest possibilities. As we agonize with you in all who
suffer pain and diminishment, so we celebrate with you in the
achievements of all who grow and create.
Amen.

January 20

Mystery Beyond Us: Praying amidst darkness

Blessed Mystery beyond us, creating and guiding us through
this changeable life, through success and disappointment,
through all the vagaries of being human, through growth
into full life and then into human illness and dissolution. We
feel you at our side and within us, and find solace from our
sorrows in your presence. You are our God, and we rejoice to
know you however slightly and uncertainly. We thank you for
life and for its ending, a totally natural and gracious event.
Amen.

January 21

You Fill The World: Hoping beyond death

Mysterious Intelligence behind everything that is, everything
that makes sense, see our heart's concerns for those we love.
You are caring and compassionate, and you fill the world
with the healing powers of nature, and put courage in human
hearts to face the diminishments that are a natural part
of being what we are. With the support of your parenting
presence, we will endure whatever discouraging and painful
elements there are in life with the hope of participating in
whatever promising events may lie ahead, ready for surprise.
Amen.

January 22

We Carry Burdens: Prayer about darkness

God of life as it is: you lay on each of us a heavy burden—
not one we can't carry, but one we at times do not enjoy
in the slightest. Death, for instance. Illness. Failure and
disappointment. Your own silence. The absolute darkness
around your being. And we add the impenetrable mystery of
violence and of absurd, meaningless events. Each of us must
carry these burdens and more, but we manage it because
our hearts have learned to choose and embrace the joys and
satisfactions of life. Grace us with a wide perspective,
Holy Creator.
Amen.

January 23

We Are Lifted: Rejoicing with food

When you give us, O Deepest Mystery, reason to rejoice
over ritual food, occasions for joy and happy remembrance,
astonishingly tasty creations out of earth's life that satisfy our
human needs perfectly, thrills discovering your unbelievably
complex and elegant creativity in animal or vegetable, we are
lifted beyond words. Exactly!
It is all literally beyond words. So hear the silent jubilation and
song of our souls, singing despite ourselves and in the dark—in
praise of you, Holy God, a song identical with our best selves.
Be thou blessed forever.
Amen.

January 24

I Am In Your Hands: Safe in God's care

One more day: it's a gift from your creating hand, Holy
Mystery. I enjoy the prospect of vital hours today, working
hours, pleasurable hours, then repose. Into your hands I
commend my spirit, parenting God, while I live another
precious day of life, perhaps a day of difficulty or of joy,
perhaps even the day I take my last human breath. I feel I am
in your hands, and—while subject to all the caprice of human
hazard and possibility—ultimately I am safe. God cares. For
this I give thanks.
Amen.

January 25

Looking Toward You: Ready for real life

Looking toward you, Creator, ever ancient, ever new, the mind and heart are humbled. We occupy so slight a plateau of time, our minds boggled by the creation around us, our hearts astonished by your generous caringness to have invented us at all. Human sadness and pain add to the mystery, but in communion with each other we know we can find strength for living through darkness until the joy of dawn returns and new hope rises in our hearts. We bless you for making us a part of this baffling existence.

Amen.

January 26

All Shall Be Well: Giving God trust

We know, Spirit Mystery, that something creative is happening in our lives all the time, something good going forward despite all we worry about. If even our worst fears came true, in your vast resources of artistry and invention would be some ultimate splendor. All shall be well: that is certainly your decree and you probably can make it happen, for you are God. Out of the greatest horrors you can bring, perhaps not every dream, but every kind of meaningful consummation.

May it be so.

Amen.

January 27

We Welcome You: In touch with God

Silent Mystery, in and around us, knowing us so much better
than we know ourselves, knowing so well the trajectory of
our talents and shortcomings, knowing our past, our present
and our plans: we welcome you into our work asking only the
intelligence to work wisely the health to enjoy it, and the heart
to carry on to success and usefulness.

Amen.

January 28

You Are Love: Rejoicing in God's love

We cannot give up on you, O God of our hearts, or abandon
our pursuit of enlightenment about your nature. You are Love:
that seems a good beginning. Your powers are limited, we
know. What can you do? What love can do, no more—but no
less either. On earth, love is supreme: all that is best in life,
most powerful and most promising—comes from love. All we
long for most—life, growth, creativity—comes from love. So
we call you "Love," and ask only that of you. But forever.

Amen.

January 29

Be Close: Prayer in trouble

Holy Mystery, God in whom we live, sorrow fills our hearts
when we face shattered dreams: beloved friends and family
taken from us by death, others in danger and in pain. Be
close to us during such times so that we can know by faith
that the shadow side of life is not without its meaning, and
our enduring it without despair shall not be without good
consequences, among them: the reward of contributing to
meaning and to beauty. All we ask is that we be given strength
to bear our life burdens in patience and in hope.
Amen.

January 30

Hear Our Prayer: Thankful for life

Holy Source of Life, our God, you give us existence minute by
minute, hour by hour, without our petitioning, and sometimes
without our gratitude. This minute we give you thanks, and
all our life and beyond we hope to do so. Hear our prayer
of appreciation: gratitude for life, for love that connects us
to others, for energy to pursue the means of further life, for
thankfulness for what we have and are. We are your grateful
creatures, Bountiful Spirit, and we dare to bless you this day.
Amen.

January 31

In Your Light: Getting strength from God

You are our source of courage, Holy Living God, companion on our life path, source of life and strength, mysterious knowing and empowering presence. In your light we know ourselves best, and in your love we feel able to face our life with all its demands and unknowns. When we must be brave, that is when we need you, not only the thought but also the reality of you. It is you who asks us and inspires us to be ourselves, our full selves, our best selves, and we can—with your help.
Amen.

FEBRUARY

February 1

We Rest In You: Resting in God

Even in our greatest bewilderment, O God, we rest in you.
Your knowledge is complete, your view is steady, your
heart never wavers. You care for us. We accept your way,
surrendering to what is and open to what shall be. With all our
race, with our departed saints and hoping in our children, we
remain faithful to our role: to live as fully as we can, to reach
out on every side to give and receive the energies of human
community, and to await in patience our life as it unfolds
within and before us.
Amen.

February 2

All Speak To Me: Finding hope

The leaves that fall, the invisible winds that blow, the
cleansing rains all speak to me of your spirit, invisible loving
Mind, Holy God, home of my heart. From childhood, we
become familiar with life's fragility, with mystery, with
earthen energies full of renewal and promise, all speaking of
the divine. So, although we find healthy doubt hovering in
our hearts, we find hope in our bones and in our bodies, with
a passion for life that knows no limitations. Ultimately you,
Holy Spirit, are our hope, our real hope, our only hope.
Amen.

February 3

Your Otherness: Noting God's remoteness

Eternal Mystery, we cannot imagine you without links to our
own remembered experience, sometimes focusing only on
your utter "otherness." Some diverse human personalities call
themselves unique, but it is you who are unique. For instance
you seem to be an Otherness when it comes to our experience
of time so we call you "eternal" though we cannot really
imagine someone existing outside of time. Thus, you once
more escape our grasp. Still you know our plight and even
planned it this way. Illumine our darkened path if there is any
way you can.
Amen.

February 4

We Are Not Begging: When praying for others

We are not begging special favors of you this day, all-
bounteous Source of Life. To those in crisis we want to say:
"You are in our prayers" but what can that mean? Beyond
a doubt you, Compassionate Spirit, are already doing
everything possible for us and for those we care about. Still,
we have the needy in our heart, and when we turn to you,
Holy God, in reverence, surrender, and gratitude, our dear
ones appear before you also. We are together in your presence,
bonded in need, just as you would have us be. May it be so.
Amen.

February 5

Another World Than This: Surrendering to God

We are slow to utter our real prayers, beloved Creator, because what we honestly hope and pray will come about is another world than this, a world much more safe with a God in it who can make everything right if only we ask. The world you have in fact given us is mysterious and full of danger, and the God in it—Thou, Holy Mystery—much too indistinct and unresponsive to the immediate yearnings in our bones. Still we surrender to the puzzling way things are, the only life we know. Be near.
Amen.

February 6

Your Heart Is Near: Trusting in God's presence

Holy Mystery at the center of all reality, whose identity is beyond our reach but whose mind and heart are near, we give thanks for your presence. We make no claim to be deep thinkers and have no need to be. Knowledge of you has always been commonplace among our race. You are simply "God," the one in whom we live and move and have our being. Beyond that we have little to go on. You give us life. You support our life. We depend on you partly because we must. Be near, Holy Mystery.
Amen.

February 7

New Promise And New Love: Finding a reason to hope

God of Mystery, not every day is a happy day for your human children. Our lives contain ambiguities, challenges, and hazards—with failure and defeat a frequent outcome, death, suffering, and chaos too frequent. But we have learned that after darkness comes the dawn, and sometimes after great pain comes a new birth, with new promise, new love, and almost endless possibility. I accept life as it shall be today taking with me the knowledge of your presence and mysterious purposes.
Amen.

February 8

Instinctual Hope: Hope even in death

Can our death, all-compassionate Mothering Spirit, like our birth, be the honored fulfillment of a natural process, as inevitable as nature, of course, but also full of expectancy? And can you provide beyond death all the acceptant love— and more—that an ideal family circle does: strong parenting love, companionable sisterly and brotherly tenderness, a world of welcome? This is our hope, God of Mystery, perhaps the wild, instinctual hope of most of your human race.
Amen.

February 9

Ocean Of Mercy: In times of failure

God our Creator, you are not only a lover of justice, full of
concern for the oppressed and the have-nots, but you are also
an ocean of mercy wherein offenders among us can find solace
and total forgiveness. You can remove our offenses from us as
far as east is from west, you can make us anew, and comfort us
in even the most profoundly blameworthy of
our deeds and omissions.
We thank you for your healing presence especially in times of
failure. May it be so.
Amen.

February 10

Elusive Creator: Finding God elusive

The continuing work of your hands, Creating God, is
prodigiously secret: why?
Why invisible, silent and easily overlooked? We can live our
daily lives as though you did not exist, and even be quite
satisfied with our superficial impressions. Could it be that
you enjoy our childish wonder, that there is beauty for you
in our stumbling rationalizations, and a communal delight in
heaven when we find you there at last? Elusive Creator, we
give thanks for the world we have though we do not begin to
understand it.
Amen.

February 11

God Of Goodness: Giving continuous thanks

Eternal Mystery, Spirit of Life and Love, God of Goodness,
our encounters with earthly wonders put us in mind of you.
All the bright side of life: the warming sun, the astonishing
animals, the nourishing plants, the people who have chosen
to be loving, grateful, and positive—sometimes in spite of
horrific difficulties—speak of their creator. Tell us something
of your name, comfort us with a sense of your surrounding
care and healing. In times of darkness, we rest in you and in
all your elusive manifestations. We give thanks continuously,
and pray for faith.
Amen.

February 12

With Unconquerable Spirit: Looking for strength in God

Humans sometimes need unconquerable spirits—a little like
your own, God of All Creation—so we can deal with illness,
tragedy, and the endless threats that are part of human life.
We are vulnerable, especially in our relationships, our links
to others. Our hearts are "out there," hoping for the best.
But so are you, Holy Mystery. If you exist at all, you exist in
vulnerability, and love implies the possibility of rejection. All
this you have created with unconquerable spirit. Companion
us in that if you can.
Amen.

February 13

Do You Share? Thoughts, on nearness, sadness, and compassion.

All-compassionate Spirit, our companioning God, do you
share in the sadness we feel when community fails, when we
engage in combat, when we fight? When—through egotism
or incaution—we do not live in peace, are you somehow
affected? Our ancestors imagined you in that way, though
impressions may misguide. Pathos is always a part of our life,
and probably therefore part of yours. We thank you for your
nearness even when we are perplexed.
Amen.

February 14

Gift Us With Gratitude: When considering living things

Living Spirit, Spirit of Life, living creatures on this earth
are astonishing: they are self-moving, self-feeding, and self-
reproducing. They use knowledge wisely, and can even reflect
on themselves and each other, remember and communicate
with each other, and create amazing art works mirroring their
own life and perspective. You have given us remarkable gifts,
have in fact made us like yourself, if ever so slightly. Gift us
with gratitude and with the vitality you hope to find well
utilized in us.
Amen.

February 15

We Ask Enlightenment: When seeking enlightenment

Loving God, human tenderness seems to blossom everywhere
if given half a chance, an awesome phenomenon, a kind of
revelation of your own mysterious goodness. It coexists in
us alongside the fierce competition of evolutionary forces,
reinforcing the mysteriousness of life, giving us pause in our
first impressions, sending us deeper, looking for an ultimate
meaning. There in the depths are you, Holy God, elusive
presence, baffling us in your creation.
We seek enlightenment.
Amen.

February 16

Our Hearts Are Restless: When looking to God

Have you somehow "made us for yourself" as Augustine
said, God of Mystery? And, as he goes on, are our hearts truly
"restless till they rest in thee"? Certainly we feel restive in
many ways. Although we rest at each day's end and awake
each morning, hopefully, rested, yet we rise to new desires,
new aims, new needs, new restlessness. Somewhere in our
soul you have planted an insatiable appetite for life, a dynamic
we experience as a deep inquietude. Is not our lifelong hope to
find rest finally in thee, in your abundance, in your very life?
May it be so.

February 17

God Invisible: When finding God in creatures

God of the wind, and like wind not visible except in your
effects, we live in the unseen force of your ongoing creativity—
this amazing cosmos, our diverse earthly human hive, the
unbelievable micro-cosmos of astonishing complexity—all of
these being effects of an unseen creative intelligence and energy:
yourself. How can we but praise you and give you our daily
worship? Teach us alertness to the revelation in all that is.
Amen.

February 18

We Worship: Searching for God

Holy God of plural gifts to us, of the many paths of human
imagination, God of the many kinds of intelligence, of
the multiple inventions of language and gesture, of the
multitudinous experiences of the human heart as it feels
the magnetic fields that surround it, we worship your
creativity in all its limitless variation and incomprehensibility.
We reverence reality, and to the extent that we can, your
wonderful and unimaginable reality. When you speak in all
that is, we shall try to listen.
Amen.

February 19

Mysterious Spirit: When mystified by God

What are we to make of your "deniability," O Mysterious
Spirit? People readily deny your existence, or pay no attention
to it at all. Is your being just another limiting illusion that
human beings are subject to? Even terrorists, while often
being believers in some sense, live within the toxic illusion
that you, Holy God, are not the God of peace and life—but are
remote, unknown and frighteningly "other." Inspire us with
prudent discernment so we may find our way in this cloud of
unknowing.
Amen.

February 20

Our Minds Into Yours: Surrendering to life

God Creator of our life, of human hearts dancing with
hope, God of falling leaves and long memory, of children
racing through days and years, of energies for hard work, of
surrendering with grace to the demands of time, we raise our
minds into yours—however slightly we can manage it—and
rejoice that life and vitality and the dynamism of relationship
throbs on and on, and we (with You) are a part of it. May your
presence teach us gratitude, and your wonders give us awe.
Amen.

February 21

Complexity Surrounds Us: When choosing not to judge

Holy Spirit Creator, at the start of a new day we turn to you in awe and need. We humans career through space together, all this quarreling, sometimes murderous, human family, lost in mystery, sometimes strong, often not. Astonishing complexity surrounds us within and without, yet illusion propels us at times into cruel judgments: this race of people I approve, this race I reject, this face I like, this one I don't. Today I will pause and try to live in this illusive truth: that darkness and light, good and evil, mix even within myself. Judge not, my soul, because you'll be wrong.

May it be so.

February 22

In The Midst Of Mystery: When hoping against hope

Holy God, hearing just a blundering prayer from us today: we greet you in lively surrender, giving in—against our drives for perfection—to the imperfections, to the flaws, of this human and earthly life we have. For reasons of your own you have invented us and have created us in a milieu that we find at times overwhelmingly sad and dangerous to lifelong sense of well being and hopefulness. Yet goodness surrounds us too, and you are its source, as you are the source of all we are. We give thanks—in the midst of mystery.

Amen.

February 23

We Look To You: Trying to have faith

Over the years, Holy God, your silence piles up. In our youth,
you took no care to make your presence clear, yet we believed.
As the time passes, your bewildering silence becomes more
burdensome; still we believe. Or perhaps "believe" is too
strong a word: we look to you. We ask, are you there? You
must be, but why is it so important to pretend not to exist?
Your challenge to us grows daily. You are our God! Help our
unbelief.
Amen.

February 24

Rejoicing In The Music: When feeling happy to exist

God of wonders, only your created music keeps us alive,
the regular rhythms of our beating hearts, the sweet up and
down melody of our forever-constant DNA patterns, the artful
harmonies of the colors our eyes see this moment. We are
filled with such music, of course, and desire to be ourselves
a kind of creative moment in the great symphony of all that
is. We rejoice at the phenomenon of repeating patterns in life,
ourselves a small but elegant configuration that fits right in
with the melody of all that is.
Amen.

February 25

Mysterious Presence: Looking to the future

Holy Mystery in whom we necessarily live and move and
have our being, you are aware of how we dread the future
because of its surprises, many unpleasant, all unknown.
Awaken your servants also to the good promises ahead along
life's path, to the joy and fulfillment and success which is our
destiny. Illuminate for us those long-range goals for which we
live: to become ourselves, to fulfill your dream of us, to enrich
the lives of those we love, to live by faith. If our heart quakes
in fear, be our comfort. If our step falters, give us strength.
Amen.

February 26

You Are Pure Mystery: Being honest with God

Dear God—an expression so many of us use with you to keep
you at a distance—because you are not "dear" in the sense that
we really hold you precious in a human sense. The truth is we
know you far too slightly to honestly cherish you as someone
"dear," and dread your presence a little too much to ever use
of you the word "precious." Instead you are Pure Mystery, and
we really know not how to address you at all. In many ways
you are simply Life, in many ways you are Death. Our God,
we are yours in fact, and yours in our desires as well.
Amen.

February 27

From Afar: Finding God incomprehensible

This day will be life's last day for thousands of human
persons, Caring Creator Spirit, and in many cases that is an
agony for everyone aware of it: for the death-bound person,
for the caregivers and everyone around. And for you, an
agony? No, unthinkable. That would imply a divine heart
in never-ending pain. Yet why not a God in never-ending
joy also sharing all human joy? Holy God, what you are is
incomprehensible to us. We cannot grasp you—nor let you go.
Holy Awesome Mysterious Presence utterly beyond us, your
creatures bless you from afar.
Amen.

February 28

You Are Able to Heal: When worried about the future

All-compassionate Spirit of the Universe, you see of course the
distress we endure in our humanness. We injure each other in
clashes of discord and misunderstanding. Disappointments
and losses weigh heavily on us. Poverty and bad choices lead
to political violence. Illness comes and remedies fail. But you
are with us this moment and always, able to dry our tears and
heal our wounds, once we have a larger perspective. Be there,
comforting Spirit. You are our hope.
Amen.

MARCH

March 1

Going To God: When thinking of death

We are all afraid to die, Holy God. We are intimidated by the
unknown, by the ultimate, by finality, by the loss of everything
familiar—because it is precisely the familiar that comforts us. But
through prayer like this, you yourself become familiar, a mystery
we speak to daily and hourly. And death can be conceived of
as simply going to you—not as anything unexpected but as our
journey's destiny from the very start of life.

May it be so.

March 2

You Accept Us: When seeking to forgive

Thank you, God, for allowing us to be imperfectly made
because it makes us, if we are wise, forgiving. Too often, too
quickly, we judge others for flawed thinking, for disguised
egotism, for rank acquisitiveness and skewed opinions. But
we can forgive them all in advance, once we accept our own
shadow side and realize how well we fit into the ranks of an
imperfect human race. You accept us, the prophets say, just as
we are—if our judgments of others are generous.

May it be so.

March 3

The One Supreme Wonder: Amazed at God's love

Behold: the spark of caring glowing for me in someone I love: it's your miracle, Creative Spirit. Could anything be more amazing? Someone loves me. Human love, however fickle and temporary, is the one supreme wonder of the world. We hold it in awe, in admiration, as if it were not of this world. I am loved? By someone I care about? Unbelievable. Beautiful beyond belief. Almost as unbelievable as yourself. God of Love, inventor of every kind of love and magnetism, we give thanks for miracles.
Amen.

March 4

You Are Shelter: Depending on God

Of course there is no way we can please everyone, Comforting Presence, my God, not only because we are full of imperfection, but also because human storms, like physical ones, sometimes come on unprovoked, and we just get caught in them. But you are shelter for us, Holy God, where we can find refuge under troubled skies. Your parenting view of us is sovereign, not dependent on others' approval; it is a positive regard, not conditioned by other circumstances. For your steady, caring hand, we are thankful.
Amen.

March 5

Your Presence Comforting: Relying on God

In times of bewilderment, we find your presence comforting,
Holy Mystery, our God. From you we come, to you we go.
And whether or not on this journey our spirit discovers your
reality at the heart of everything, there you are nevertheless,
moving us from within toward our destiny. You cannot not
be present, you cannot not be active in us and around us. We
entrust ourselves to the forces that carry us along our life's
path, and put our ultimate reliance on you.
Amen.

March 6

Ourselves On Your Side: Siding with God

Holy God, constantly spoken to in human prayers all over the
earth, implored for help in every crisis and need, we simply
want to be in solidarity with people praying everywhere, and
to place ourselves on your side, wherever that is. It must be
the side of justice, of intelligent and rational thought, and of
those religious claims that are based on honesty and reverence.
We revere what is known for certain about you, and for all that
is unknown: your name, for instance, and your essence. Keep
us from spiritual illusion, Holy God, and in compassion with
all who share with us this Cloud of Unknowing.
Amen.

March 7

We Turn To You: Thoughts of death

Holy Creator, how can we accept and surrender to the disappointments and illnesses that come our way—when our culture endorses only success, affluence, and endless health? Even when we hear Sister Death approaching and eventually knocking on our door, we find very few supports around us. Then we turn most readily to you. Then we shall ask that, as you accompany us through each of life's days, you be there when shadows fill our horizon. We trust that you will. May it be so.

March 8

You Hear Every Word: When unable to pray

As you know so well, kindly Creator Spirit, often we are not focused enough to pray, to really communicate with you, to speak into your silence. Our life can be chaotic, with concentration impossible. Still our hearts pray, our bodies pray, our spirits pray—if only in their intractable orientation toward life and peace of mind. In many ways Desire is our name, and our essence. You, dear Mystery, in the penetrating perceptions of your intelligence, know us utterly, and hear every voiceless word and utterance of our hearts.
We give thanks.
Amen.

March 9

Death In The Air: Thinking of death

So dangerous is this planet-home of ours, Cosmic Inventor
God, Spirit within everything, that bodily death—just as truly
as life—is always in the air. Our accommodations here are
temporary, a fact easily overlooked unless we are in touch
with our group memory, our keepers of history, and our circles
of fellowship. Death turns us to the thought of you, Invisible
Presence, and gives us motivation to accomplish some
meaningful work before it's all over. Be with us in that.
Amen.

March 10

Cloud of Unknowing: In times of pain

This is obviously not a world you totally control, Spirit of Life:
that is surely your own mysterious decree. So while you are
the ultimate source of all that is (and for that we honor you),
there are insoluble mysteries in the chaotic way things are, and
you expect us to live with these without further explanation.
So be it. The conventional rationalizations of pain and evil do
not really seem plausible, so with your help we hold to our
faith in your presence despite this Cloud of Unknowing in
which you have placed us.
Amen.

March 11

We Are Baffled: When tempted against faith

Holy Mystery beneath and within all that is, we are baffled
by the contradiction between your colossal creation—in all
its beauty and elegance—and the phenomenon of evil within
that creation. These two contradictory realities are constantly
mind boggling, inclining us to give up either our confidence in
human thought or our instinctual faith in your existence and
sovereign goodness. For today, we still cling to both—since
we have both intelligence that we must respect and hearts that
cannot despair. Guide us, if you can, on our precarious way
forward in faith.
Amen.

March 12

We Cannot Name You: Not knowing God's essence

Spirit-Sophia, Holy God, as we look toward you and
awkwardly "name toward" you, your essence remains
so far beyond our words and even our imagination (but
not our faith). We rejoice in your existence and in your
companionship, in your nourishing light and your quickening
presence, and we give thanks you have brought us into this
moment where, pooling energies with you, we can make our
unique contribution to life and enjoy the thrill of a meaningful,
powerful existence.
Amen.

March 13

My Being Speaks: To exist is to pray

When my mind is far from concentration and my heart unfocused, still my being speaks to you, God of life, God of promise. There is hope for me because you are a caring creator, and have filled our experience with caring. There are links of concern and love in my own heart for those around me, and energies of love from others to me. In such a circle we can survive, and with imagination can find joy in the mysterious dance of daily life with all its unknowns and challenges.
Amen.

March 14

If You Whisper: Fellowship with the divine mystery

If you whisper my name today, Creating Spirit, like young Samuel, I would answer: "Speak, Lord, for thy servant heareth"—except that you seem less a "lord" than a servant yourself. In your elusive liveliness, you seem unable to give lord-like commands, and seem more like someone open to reasonable requests, happy to make life productive of all we need for survival today, though earthly life is, like everything, impermanent. Speak, then, Servant Spirit, for thy fellow servant heareth.
Amen.

March 15

Can We Trust You?: Considering the mystery of your parentage

Mystery of Intelligence all around us, holding the world
together by constant speeds, measured heat, and energy
systems infinitely complex and sure, do you also look on us
with affection, concern, pride, and warm-hearted love? Are
you father-like? Can we ultimately trust you? As we confront
the darkness amidst blinding light, may we also rest in your
caring? Are you our loving parent, worrisome, burdened with
the uncertainty in our freedom? Be our God today.
Amen.

March 16

Be Close: When disappointment comes

Holy Mystery, God in whom we live, sorrow fills our hearts
when we face shattered dreams, beloved friends and family
taken from us by death, others in danger and in pain. Be close
to us during such times so that we can know by faith that
the shadow side of life is not without its meaning, and our
enduring it shall not be without its reward. All we ask is that
we be given strength to bear our life burdens in patience and
in hope. May we somehow find strength to carry on to the end
in communion with our fellow humans.
Amen.

March 17

Hear Our Prayer: Why we bless God

You give us existence minute by minute, hour by hour,
without our petitioning, and sometimes without our
awareness, Holy Source of Life, our God, our Meaning. This
minute we give you gratitude, and for all our life and beyond
we hope to continue to do so. Hear our prayer of thanks: for
life, for love that connects us to others, for energy to pursue
the means of further life, for appreciation of what we have and
are. We are your grateful creatures, bountiful Spirit, and we
dare to bless you this day.
Amen.

March 18

In Your Light: When in need of courage

You are our source of courage, Holy Living God, companion
on our life path, source of life and strength, mysterious
knowing and empowering presence. In your light we know
ourselves best, and in your love—and the love of our fellow
humans—we feel able to face our life with all its demands.
When we must be brave, that is when we need you. It is you
who asks us to be courageously ourselves, our full selves, our
best selves, and we can—with your help.
Amen.

March 19

We Rest In You: When resting in God

In our greatest bewilderment, O God, we rest in you. Your knowledge is complete, your view is steady, your heart never wavers. We accept your way, surrendering to what is and open to what shall be. With all our race and with our saints in holy remembrance, we remain faithful to our role: to live as fully as we can, to reach out on every side, to give and receive support, and to accept our life as it unfolds within and before us, forgiving ourselves our shortcomings and enjoying the clownish excesses of our egotism.
Amen.

March 20

The World We Know: Hoping in darkness

The world we know, the earthen scene, Creator Spirit, is shamefully full of starving people, abused women and children, unjustly imprisoned men, hoarded resources, a depleted environment, stockpiled weapons—and blind guides. Without exaggeration, the human milieu is, in many perspectives, tragic and destined for tragedy. Yet each day promising infants are born, young minds open and search, fresh hands take up leadership, dreaming of making life different, especially for the most deprived. Your creation can save itself, and we can help. May it be so.
Amen.

March 21

We Simply Give Thanks: Thanks for what is

God of mystery and unimaginable inventiveness, who has created each of us in all our beauty and potential energies, we simply give thanks this day for what we are and for what we have, for our own mysterious life forces and our hopes for life ahead. We simply give thanks to be and to be ourselves and to be linked to those we love. Give us courage for the unique life journey that is ours, energies for the work we must do, and hearts full of personal courage and encouragement for our earthly companions.
Amen.

March 22

Nothing Is Fixed: Praying while in motion

The clock ticks, Holy God of the cosmos, marking the daily spin of our earth into and out of the sun's light. The calendar grows slowly obsolete, measuring out the annual journey of the earth around its day-star and the course of our own ups and downs. Nothing is fixed. Everything is in motion— even our soul's advance into destiny. What a privilege to be a participant in it all, part of why it all exists, part of the appreciative audience before the mysterious symphony of existence.
Amen.

March 23

We Wonder: Praying even in doubt

We wonder at times, God of All, if ever a single prayer of ours reached your heart, if our bubbling ego or frequent self-deception may not have blocked our words from authenticity or flooded out the delicate shoots of our growing, honest faith. But then the thought of your communicativeness, of the generosity you so thoroughly displayed in creating anything at all, calms our fears, and we see that simply because you are God all the longings of your creatures are in your caring concern. We give thanks for that.
Amen.

March 24

In Your Hands: God known and unknown

Holy, Unknown Mystery we call "God," you give us evidence of your intimate presence with us in the mysterious laws of nature. Without fail light has a fixed speed, hearts beat at a regular pace, magnetism holds earth in predictable orbit, the earth itself orbited by a constant moon. We are in your hands—but who are you, Nameless Spirit? Not so much a "someone" as the very ground of existence, a virtually unknowable being, beyond our comprehension altogether. We are simply in awe of your presence everywhere.
Amen.

March 25

Holy Darkness: Reaching beyond reality

We long, Holy Darkness, Wild Brilliance too bright to see, for more life, for more knowledge, for more love all around and within us, for final escape from mortality and into eternal time at last. We long for the impossible also: to fly, to win every competition, to comprehend the holy mysterious around us. Does all this longing—as involuntary as our next gasp for air—achieve anything? It is the best we can do. Accept it as our prayer for today.
Amen.

March 26

Why Aren't You Almighty?: Praying our wild wishes

God of Immense Goodness, prayers arise from our hearts even when our heads tell us it's futile. Our reasoning is correct, but our instinct overrides it: you are God, why won't you help? You are all-good, why aren't you all-mighty? Surely wishful thinking (that you were all-mighty) is not totally bad—provided we can laugh at ourselves, and revere your sovereignty, along with your deep compassion and the incalculable outpouring of love that this creation is—prior to any prayers of ours to improve it. May it be so.
Amen.

March 27

Every Kind of Love: When searching for magic

Holy Inventor of Life, we rejoice when the sparks of human
love flash in our darkened world and we catch a glimpse
of the real magic within creation. Awesome is physical
magnetism, and the magnetism we know as friendship,
but bodily and sexual magnetism is a unique wonder:
from it comes new human life and human community and
tomorrow's entire world. Every kind of love provides a
metaphor for your own divine being, and we are in awe.
Amen.

March 28

By Great Luck: Giving thanks for love

When we thank you for our existence, Holy God, we do
accept creation merely as it is: a most promising potential, an
evolving community of living things, an unknown destiny.
Love, by great luck, is our birthright; love is our lifelong study;
love is our home, and we build it from our earliest days. We
thank you for our world of caring that grows and blossoms.
And while love seems lasting, human life itself is not: that is
temporary and fragile. We do thank you for the love, and we
do accept this good, fleeting life as it is.
Amen.

March 29

Too Many Unknowns: Our part in giving thanks

Holy Creator, no matter how focused and alert we may be,
we are incapable of really appraising the infinite ocean of
blessings that have come to us from your generous hands: they
are incalculable. In our limited vision some of us seem to be
more blessed than others—so our imperative is to share with
others what we have. Possibly all of us must say, in the final
analysis, that our God-given gifts are rich beyond measure,
and join in earth's song of eternal thanksgiving.
May it be so.
Amen.

March 30

In Desperate Need: Wishing for more

O God of infinite wealth, we are in desperate need—but your
wealth is creative love and most of the time we forget our need
for it as we suffer the anguish over our other human needs:
for work success, for the safety of children and loved ones, for
food, for shelter. Your bountiful hands offer—besides our very
being and all our energies—what you can give us: boundless
positive regard. It is a love that is divine and spiritual: excuse
us if at times we wish it felt more human and palpable.
Amen.

March 31

Faith In Life: Thanks for life

Thanks for the grace of faith in life, generous God. However deep the shadows, the central scene on earth is bright: you care for us, you hold us in being, you are present in the promise that is always a part of life. Something tells us all shall be well: is it the rising bright sun? The drama of growing things? The flavor of oranges? The speed of light? Our world is alive with evidence of your mysterious presence and we are grateful to be aware of the wonders around us, all invisible and silent as most of them are.

Amen.

APRIL

April 1

We Give Worship: The wonders around us

God of wonders: at civil celebrations multi-color fireworks,
sparkling and noisy, astonish our eyes and ears. They seem
spectacular beyond belief. Still they are no match for the simple
miracle of wild flowers exploding daily, colorful eye-popping
designs (which bloom everywhere at our feet) and which are
actually alive and can even reproduce themselves before it is
time to die—while fireworks have no life of their own, and are
gone in seconds. We give worship to the One who invented it
all, with thanks for the wonders humans make, and the miracles
that flow directly from you, Holy Creator.
Amen.

April 2

The Beauty Of Children: Praying amid ambiguity

The stunning beauty of children mirrors your mystery, Holy
God, a beauty occasioning greater awe when we think what
will be asked of them: the same mortal life we have, edged
with disappointment and sown with sorrow and pain, but
promising joy too, and creative in thousands of ways. Creator
Spirit, ultimate inventor of the way things are, why can there
not be pure ecstasy in human life? Why must there be so much
unfairness and free decision-making with its potential for evil
consequences? We are baffled. Come to our aid.
Amen.

April 3

We May Speak Plainly: Trusting in God

Dear God, we know we may speak plainly to you because of
your intimacy with our every thought. You are completely
familiar with our life, our failures, and our frailty. None of us
is made of stone or steel, of alabaster or ivory. We are people of
flesh and blood, flesh that carries scars, blood that easily pulses
beyond control. You know us well—far better than we know
ourselves. So in your presence we need not be formal. Beloved
Mystery, then, be near. Without our faith in your caring, we are
without hope either. We put our trust in you.
Amen.

April 4

Guide Us, Creator: Being inspired by God's love

Are those mystics correct who say we should make ourselves
into an incarnation of you, Mysterious Spirit, an in-the-flesh
agent of the divine heart? "You have no hands on earth but
ours," prayed mystic Teresa of Avila. That might lay too heavy
a burden on us, to see and meet people the way you yourself
would, to care for their pain, for their needs. Yet how else
will your heart have its way? Guide us, Creator of Light and
Wisdom. Make us—as much as you can—instruments of your
love.
Amen.

April 5

Extremes of Pain: Praying in despair and sadness

It is in the extremes of pain, Holy Mystery, in the torture of
serious illness and of ongoing tragedy, that we lose faith. Be
with us, support our hearts as they break all unexpectedly,
as they reach out in vain to save those we love. Tragedy so
incomprehensible—as you are incomprehensible yourself. Why
must human life be so agonizing, so unsatisfactory, for so many?
Save us from despair, Holy Spirit, if you can. We want to put our
faith in you. As you have already brought wonders into being,
we entrust to you the remedies and healing of all that is evil.
Amen.

April 6

You Are The Great Spirit: Prayer of high expectations

You have been our God in the past, Holy Mystery, though
we often mis-imagined you. You are the Spirit we admire
and worship now beneath this colossal creation around us.
But mostly you are the Great Invisible Wind-like Mystery,
unknown and unnamable, who draws us toward a world
of justice and love, toward hope, toward creativity, and
an energetic life. We thank you for all you promise as you
reassure us of your caring, speaking to the silent expectations
of our hearts. You are our God: we revere you and all the work
of your hands and heart.
Amen.

April 7

We Gain Balance: Praying about death

May we call upon the dead, Holy God, to bless us with
their mystery? To do so would be just to join in the requiem
and yearning lament of our race since earthly time began.
Honoring death is one thing that makes us identifiably human.
Hear our prayer, then, God of life and death. Somehow we
know you still, even in years of aging and diminishment.
Perhaps that is because we are approaching your mystery as
we, alas, know you best: in death. We gain balance when we
celebrate life, but every life we know leads to dissolution. Be
God of both to us, Holy Presence.
Amen.

April 8

A Privilege to Believe: The healing uses of faith

It is a special privilege, Holy Mystery, to believe in you. It
creates at last a world that makes sense. You are Creativity: a
quality we also can experience in ourselves, if ever so slightly.
You love your creations: we also know what that is like.
Your creations are beyond our understanding: but that is not
unexpected. What is also beyond us is death, sorrow, pain and
disappointment. We surrender in faith to the unknown, to you.
The movement and forces within this evolving world envelop
us, but amid it all we hold on to you, to your holy presence. Be
there always: and for that I thank you in advance.
Amen.

April 9

This Earthly City: Hoping without end

It is this earthly city, Holy Creating Spirit, that we are building.
It is here that we are blossoming and becoming our full selves,
drawing others into the comforting circle of life, especially
those who may otherwise be left outside. Open my heart, Holy
Mystery, so I may in turn find someone open to me. Religion
starts here in community, in extraordinary diversity, rich in
unknowns. Still our hearts are restless with the unexpected,
and perhaps that is because we are created full of tomorrow,
endlessly hopeful that life, like hope, may be itself endless.
May it be so.

April 10

Preserve Us: Prayer growing into action

Preserve us if you can, Holy Mystery, from the darkness
of mere wishful thinking—and give us instead the bright
morning light of honest acceptance of things as they are,
especially their temporality, and particularly the reality of
human vulnerability to illness and to inevitable death. Despite
the unknowns, you expect us to live a life of hope, of solidarity
with others, and with belief in your benevolence toward
us despite all worries to the contrary. If it seems that some
humans are less blessed than others, give us the graciousness
to sometimes be ourselves their blessing. May it be so.
Amen.

April 11

Goodness Reigns: The grace that abounds

Your creativity, Holy God, astonishes us—and is meant to. We
thank you for wonder, and for wondrous things: the beauty
and promise of children, the vitality and idealism of young
people, love as it blossoms and buds into new life, all the
courage and ebullience of human thriving, and finally the
wisdom and humility of elders. Evil forces have their day, but
goodness reigns in the long run. We read: "Where sin abounds,
grace does more abound." Hope is available for us in the
hearts of a circle of the faithful. We give thanks for it all.
Amen.

April 12

We Live with Dread: Living with uncertainty

Because you have created us such passionate lovers, God of
Mystery, we live with dread also, the underside of love. The
sweet satisfactions of beauty and caring can draw us into
illusions. "Perhaps we can keep this treasured thing forever!"
says enthusiasm. "Perhaps this precious moment will stay!" says
our heart. But our wiser self knows it's less than true. Instead
you expect us to surrender to both love and dread. Heavy-
hearted, we accept the impermanence of time, hoping none the
less for what prophets have spoken of, some kind of eternal
life following this one. May it be so.
Amen.

April 13

We Need Faith: A prayer about meaning

Mysterious God of all creation, we need faith in you if only
to make us wise about life, the earth, and especially about
the needy. Faith in you gives us perspective, for with faith we
can imagine things as you see them. Suddenly our hearts are
expanded to take in every living human, the astounding world
of animal life, and the earth and cosmos itself. By faith we may
begin to see with your eyes—and everything is different. There
is meaning in each color and shape, in each sound and motion,
in everything that is. May it be so.
Amen.

April 14

Beyond Comprehension: Prayer of hope in darkness

Holy Source of Life, every quality of your being is beyond my
comprehension. I give thanks to you because you are good
to me, and good to all that exists, to all that lives. Evil, pain,
disappointment, tragedy, and illusion abound—we know not
why—but the graciousness of life abounds infinitely more:
an endless abundance. All that exists is essentially good, and
beautiful, and true, and promising—if we have perspective—
and faith. Grant us that light in this darksome world where so
many struggle forward without enlightenment or a reason for
hope.
Amen.

April 15

Into the Silence: Praying into the silence

In your profound silence, Holy Mystery, we hear a call to faith. Beyond the sorrow and disappointment in life, deep in the fabric of things, there is a blessing: the blessing of existence, of having been chosen to be, of the challenge to become wiser and more useful to the community. At some point in the past our name was called, and here we are, one of the blessed ones who exist. May our heart's reply to your call each day be "I am here" and our determination strengthened to carry on—in the darkness, speaking bravely and confidently into your profound silence.
Amen.

April 16

You Are The Meaning: Giving thanks for life

You are present in the deepest pleasures of life, Holy Creating Spirit, marking us as more than accidental life forms but as persons made for joy, for meaningful happiness. You are in the ecstasy, in the fun, in the camaraderie, in the excitement, in the music, in the banqueting, in the dance, in the peace at day's end. More than that, you are in the meaning of it all: your love made it happen and for a purpose. We give thanks— inadequately but the best we are capable of. May your holy way come about on this earth, and throughout the universe.
Amen.

April 17

Beloved Mystery: Praying God's presence

It is not only your existence but your presence, Holy
Mysterious, that centers reality for us. You are not just
theoretical, you are alive, you know us perfectly and care
infinitely: you are transcendently present. For our part, we
can reach our destiny only with that vibrant atmosphere
around us, your being, your immediacy, and your love. In this
environment our faith is born and grows, and our life forever
has a center. yourself, beloved Mystery. May it be so always,
today and through all the foreseeable and unforeseeable
future.
Amen.

April 18

Fill Our Hearts: Feeling touched by God

Holy Mysterious Creator, source of life and of consciousness,
we pray today in the ancient words of the Hindu Upanishads,
preserved for many centuries because of their beloved
inspiration and uncommon faith. "O God, lead us from death
to life, from falsehood to truth. Lead us from despair to hope,
from fear to trust, from hate to love, from war to peace. Let
peace fill our hearts, our world, and our universe." Heartfelt
are these words: may my own heart be moved by such
inspiration. This ancient faith seems as alive today as ever.
May it be so.
Amen.

April 19

Some questions have no answer, dear Spirit of Unthinkable
Mystery, and one of them is "Why is there something rather
than nothing?" We might say: "Because our God is good"—but
who grasps what we're talking about? "Goodness pours itself
out," we may also say, and even on a human level we know
our creative self, our out-going self is our best self. But that
such goodness be the very source of absolutely everything:
can we think that thought? God of Goodness, be near. Be our
enlightenment, our hope, and our courage.
Amen.

April 20

Be With Us: Asking for wisdom

What is the purpose of human life, all-knowing Creating
Mystery? If we could discern it, we could take up that purpose
and make it our aim too. Or can we even ask such a question?
It presumes we find meaning in at least some of what happens.
It assumes we can know enough about life to get a sense of its
parameters. And if we suspect that yet another life happens
after this one is over, our answer will be categorically different.
Holy God, what is this world about, a limited lifetime that
ends permanently and totally, or a prelude to an eternal life?
Be with us. To deal with these questions, we need a wisdom
far beyond the ordinary.
Amen.

April 21

As we notice life appearing on this earth wherever it can,
Holy Source of All Life, so it seems likely that living things,
amazing to behold, must occur on other masses flying through
space—wherever possible. Your creation is mind-boggling
enough just on this earth, but when we imagine your creation
throughout space—those billions of distant entities in all their
wild patterns and complexities—our mind is baffled. But
our hearts continue to bless you, God of All, and the work of
your energies near and far. Be near, be our guiding spirit in
everything.
Amen.

April 22

Warm Our Hearts: Praying for light

Holy Fire at the heart of reality, warm our human hearts with
the energies of passion and compassion, illuminate our minds
with the truth of our temporary and mortal state, and give us
a hint of enlightenment about the purpose of our existence.
Illuminate for us the world with all its awesome wonders, so
we may go about our life wisely and modestly, ready to reject
illusions, ready to accept facts however harsh, grateful for the
honor of being part of it all. Give us enough human wisdom to
cope with the gift of this astonishing life itself.
Amen.

April 23

Send Prophetic People: Praying for peace

How heartbreaking to you, Divine Womb of Life, must be the
sounds of war. Your beloved children on each side thrown
murderously against each other for reasons they do not really
comprehend—often by leaders who value egotism above life.
Send us prophetic people, Holy One, men and women who can
turn our hearts toward negotiation, toward peace, tolerance,
and civilization—lest the killing wars continue and thousands
more die needlessly. It cannot be your will that so much violence
prevail, or that the strong and lucky dominate. Grace us with
leaders who love and revere the challenge of making peace.

Amen.

April 24

You Love Us: Praying without words

I feel sure, Holy Presence, that my every failed attempt to
find prayerful words—is a prayer. You did not empower us
to be good at speaking into silence, carrying on a one-way
conversation with you, as it were. Instead, our hearts speak,
our actions speak, our patience and perseverance and good
intentions speak, and eloquently. You hear the voice of our
inarticulateness, and you are praised by it—for we have not
despaired or given up. Your perfect compassion hears our
desire, and you love us for it, no doubt, for we are the work of
your hands. May it be so.

Amen.

April 25

Give Us Wisdom: Prayer without fear

We give thanks, Loving Mystery, that we live in a milieu
essentially benevolent—where our most evil adversaries are
ultimately only humans like ourselves, not super-powerful
evil spirits. They can be successfully opposed by patience, by
faith, by education and communion. With your help, human
community can grow up strong and inspiring around us as
protection from the false consciousness of superstition and
imaginary threats. Give us a worldwide, communal wisdom,
Holy Spirit, and a calming awareness of your gracious
presence.
Amen.

April 26

You Hide From Us: Finding God beneath everything

You hide from us, Invisible Presence, Holy God, for reasons
of your own, yet we find you nonetheless: as Planner
beneath otherwise baffling "laws" holding the natural world
together, as Answer to otherwise unanswerable questions—
like "Why is there something rather than nothing?" Your
evolutionary design of the evolving world shines out from
within everything: your breathtaking ingenuity everywhere
is awesome. We praise you, however inadequate our voices
seem, and however far we are from full comprehension of
what's going on. The world is ultimately safe in your hands.
Amen.

April 27

Our Prayer Without Words: Praying beyond words

God of All, we turn to you this day in gratitude to be alive,
knowing all we are and have is from you, wanting to pray
as religious people have always done. But nothing comes:
no words at all. It is all too complicated. What can we use
for utterances when our minds draw a blank? It is at times
just like this, Holy Presence, that without words our prayer
goes forth—in our soundless good desires and persevering
decisions. And you (in your soundless delight in us) reply—
with continued life, with some measure of courage, and with
our gracious life energies. May it be so.
Amen.

April 28

God Beyond Names: Expression of prayerful unknowing

Your mysteriousness deepens, God of our hearts, when we
consider the problem of naming you, and therefore of thinking
of you deeply. Superficially we call you "God" and feel we
know what we are talking about—until we reflect that you
could not be a lonely, single entity—like "a God"—but have to
also experience relationships, since that is the nature of every
personal entity we know of. Or are you somehow impersonal?
Or in-between? God beyond our names and our thoughts, we
bless you anyway, in a kind of sacred unknowing.
Amen.

April 29

God Almost Unbelievable: Praying despite unbelief

Out of the depths of bewilderment, almost unbelievable Deity,
and in the comforting presence of each other, we turn to you.
You are totally unbelievable to some,—and you are almost
unbelievable to others, those whose experience of life includes
mysteries so full of elegance, they are tempted to distrust their
evidence. There are still others who feel the world around us
contains too many tragedies to be the work of a God. To all
humans, you are—if you exist—beyond us. Into the darkness of
your mystery, into the silence, we speak. Help thou our unbelief.
Amen.

April 30

We Cannot Understand: Giving thanks in darkness

We think of you, God, as "Holy Mystery" because we cannot
begin to understand you: an intelligence and force who
fashioned this intricate, evolving web of human life, and
created the spinning ball of earth whereon we live and travel
through space—to say nothing of the miraculous phenomenon
of love and altruism, the magnetism of affection, that bonds
us so beautifully to each other and draws us into procreation,
family, and community. You are the Miracle and Unidentifiable
Sweetness beneath and behind all that is. We give you praise
and gratitude.
Amen.

MAY

May 1

Be With Us: Praying despite darkness

Holy Silent Creating Spirit behind all that is, we are mystified by evil in our world. Perhaps the frightening force we call "the big bang" can explain the threat we continuously feel from volcanoes, tsunami, and asteroids; or perhaps the force we call "evolution" can rationalize the unforgiving violence among animals, the evils of disease, and death. But why the heartbreak and gratuitous agony of so many children and innocents, why the promise in human energies so often frustrated? Be with us, O God, in this darkness.

Amen.

May 2

We Reach Out: Addressing an unknowable God

Mysterious Creating Presence, are prayers essentially nonsensical? How can we speak to you at all when we cannot really imagine an Entity that cannot be named, that cannot even be counted—so that there would be but one of you, one solitary divine being, not two and therefore not burdened by the disadvantage of feeling "alone"? Is not a "Lonely God" as grotesque as a Monkey God? Through the darkness we reach out to you in metaphor. Hear our prayer and enlighten and encourage our hearts.

Amen.

May 3

Come To Our Minds: Speaking into mystery

Speak to us, great Mystery, in whatever words we can really
hear: through the written wisdom of the past, through our
understandings of present events, and through the silence
of the future—but also through pain and adversity and the
unexpected, and in all the wild democracy of our human
differences. The elegance glistening within physical reality is
also a language, but one we do not fully comprehend. Speak:
your servants are listening. Come, enlighten our minds,
Creator Spirit, though your utterances may be baffling.
Amen.

May 4

All Images Fail: Searching for knowledge of God

Friendly Presence, creator of all that is, we find that it is in
linking with others that we find our way into our best selves.
Is your divine being also communitarian in some way? Is your
essence a Solitude or a Communion? Of course all images fail
in our attempts to comprehend you, but some comparisons
give us light, however dim. Perhaps you can be thought of as
a multiplicity of liveliness. Not two, not three, but not solitary
either: a force, an atmosphere, like an unseen wind, like an
ever-present parent. Guide us in our search for you, holy
indescribable Creator.
Amen.

May 5

We Have Lost Them: Praying despite tragedy

Nothing worse could a people bear, God of life, than of sudden death for thousands of innocents, in a flash, in a hundred-story crash and instantaneous extinguishing. Our hearts almost die, disbelieving. Never was such horror known, even in imagination, before. We have lost them: without a face to admire one last time, without eyes to close in death, without time to let go. The vast wound is vastly raw, admitting no balm. Is your heart still with us, infinite Life? We trust it is. Your mystery of your goodness continues to glow beneath and around us. Be near.
Amen.

May 6

Different Mysteries: Questioning the mystery of God

Holy Creator, source of life and being, we are always in search of you. Why are our efforts so fruitless? You seem to have invented here a world where you can remain perfectly invisible, almost unnecessary, and seemingly inaccessible. Are there perhaps other worlds where you experiment with different mysteries? Are there, out in your cosmos somewhere, intelligent persons or spirits who hear your unmistakable voice of care, guidance, and encouragement and know explicitly all your desires? Ours is a harder way, but so be it.
Amen.

May 7

Love Is Real: Honoring the God of love

God of Wisdom: we thank you for inspired thinkers whose insight can guide us through the dark. We need fresh clarity every day. This life is temporary, this world is insecure. What matters most—we know instinctively—is love, our caring for one another, our delight in everything beautiful, love, the supreme phenomenon in human life. If anything is real, then, it is love, itself the best paradigm for our creator. You are, like love, what is the most real though the least provable: your divine self within us, at our side, at our destiny, a loving God, our Source and our Home. Thank you for being there, here, and everywhere.
Amen.

May 8

What Can We Trust: Praying God's mystery

What can we rely on, Holy Mystery, except the Solid Ground that you are? Unlike the earthly ground we walk on—that seems so permanent, but isn't—you alone supposedly never change—at least in faith's first conception. An earthquake is disorienting because the earth under us seems ultimate, the one thing that cannot move. But that impression is false. You alone are ultimate, unchangeable, the foundation even of our thought. It is you we trust in, you we must learn to remember and depend on, despite your invisibility and pervasive silence.
Amen.

May 9

It is ragtag human company you keep, Creating Mystery,
merciful mother of lepers and human outcasts, ultimate father
of thieves and rascals, sister-brother to the marginalized,
the halt and blind, the deaf and the ill, a god of humans
full of need, and forever pursuing illusions and rumors, yet
"immortal diamonds" are we, each of us, in the poet's phrase.
You have us as you made us: imperfect, crudely shaped, dull
of mind—but full of promise, every single one of us. Give us
insight and gratitude for things as they are.

Amen.

May 10

Teach us to pray, Holy Mystery, in a way that is honest. "Ask
and you shall receive," said Jesus of Nazareth. When we do
this, do we believe that we are praying to a male father figure
in the sky? Does this affect what we pray for? Perhaps we are
better off with images that leave us free of social prejudice,
better off with vague impressions more true to our experience:
our Source, the Ground of Being, the Mind that energizes the
universe. You are the loving mystery at the heart of all that is:
we give you thanks for this astonishing and lucky existence.

We pray that you would teach us to pray honestly.

Amen.

May 11

Without Answers: When feeling in darkness

Holy Creator of all we know, you expect us to live without answers to many fundamental questions: who are we human beings? What were we born to do? Where are we going, individually and corporately? How shall we live together wisely? To all these questions, you seem to be yourself a major factor in the answer: you have made us for yourself, your generosity is our model, your world of eternal life is our destiny. Yet you yourself are incomprehensible to our human minds. You dwell in mystery. We live therefore in darkness, having faith that all is well, or will be made well in the long run. May it be so.

Amen.

May 12

Surrounded By Beauty: When grateful for what is

Nothing more enlivens us than does beauty, God Artist of All Creation: the beautiful face, the powerful body, the graceful, expressive voice, a golden dawn, the rainbow half-circling the sky, the harmony of life forms, the sun setting over mountains, the starry night, the innocence and vivaciousness of children. You surround us with beauty—if we take time to see and hear it and take it in: above and beneath us, behind and ahead of us. Our life can be awesome; grace us to live it wisely, finding beauty wherever we go. May it be so.

Amen.

May 13

Spirit in a Church: When needing community

Is it not your very Spirit that draws people together, Holy
Creator, into circles, cultures and nations, as churches, as
groups, and as families? We have learned over years and
millennia that it is only when we are together, we are each our
best selves. Only in being in community can we find the way
ahead, can we find enlightenment. Only in human communion
are we truly creative and procreative. We thank you for that
spirit, and reach out for ever more of it.
Amen.

May 14

Differences Fascinate: Appreciating God's mystery

Few things in life fascinate us, Mysterious Creator God, more
than the differences, the wild diversity we experience language
to language, mind to mind, body to body, species to species.
We can never be completely at rest while along our path we
can choose to take bridges to unknown territory waiting
to be explored. We are born explorers, born students, born
adventurers, born seekers, born contemplatives. We give you
thanks, Holy God, most fascinating enigma and mystery of all,
to the understanding of whom every created thing is a bridge.
Amen.

May 15

Equal Rights Fundamental: When needing gender balance

Few elements of our world are more confusing than "gender,"
Creator of this abundant life, yet you require that we live
with the confusion. Beyond a doubt, equal rights for the sexes
is a fundamental requisite in an enlightened society, yet an
eccentric culture can affect us negatively and make us sexists,
subconsciously preferring one gender to another. In your
creating presence we shall honor fundamental rights that go
deeper than culture, respecting the voices and opinions of all
parties, seeking illumination for our searching and vulnerable
hearts, regardless of deep differences among us.
Amen.

May 16

Friendly Spirit: When feeling a surge of hope

It is our hope that you, Holy God, look at us the way our true
friends do, with acceptant and positive regard, with love for us
just the way we are, with unshakable concern for our welfare. Is
that too much to hope for? Yet nothing is really too much to hope
for—in a world where love seems to be woven into the fabric
of every personal heart, and beauty is everywhere—despite
undeniable defects as well. So do we hope in you, Friendly
Spirit. You are with us always, and we thank you for that.
Amen.

May 17

Beyond Qualities: Feeling in God's presence

Unnamable Mystery and Meaning beneath all that is, we
have assumed too long that your name is "Almighty God."
What does it mean to be all-mighty? If you were "almighty"
as humans understand the word, would you not protect your
beloved creatures more perfectly, especially when they beg for
help from you? Perhaps "All Compassionate" is a name closer
to the truth—but no name even begins to identify you, so
unknown are you to minds like ours. Whatever word we use
to name you—fails. You are a Presence: and that describes our
experience. May it be so.

Amen.

May 18

No One Go Hungry: Longing to reach out to others

We give thanks today, world's Creator, that the earth we
animals tread on is also a fertile womb that produces green
vegetables and refreshing fruit, trees we build into shelter,
and water for a thousand purposes. Abundance is earth's
theme: food is plentiful. How inept of us to fail to distribute it
efficiently to those it is created for. But this is your trumpet call
to world unity: only cooperating—not competing—can we be
sure no one shall go hungry. May we grow in this unity more
with each passing day.

Amen.

May 19

When we cannot pray at all, friendly divine Presence, God of all that is—in illness or exhaustion or depression—our very distress calls out to you, and you are there. You are never without care for us, and if our instincts are correct, the greater our distress, the greater is your caring. We are caught in the pain of evolution's unfolding and suffer—as if in childbirth—as the future is born: yet you are always with us, welcoming us into our unknown destiny. May it be so.

Amen.

May 20

Holy Mysterious Creator, God of Justice, when we ask ourselves "Why does anything exist?" we can only reply, "Because of the generosity and goodness of God." We call it goodness, but that does not begin to encompass our amazement at creation's plentitude. Gratitude is our feeble response, but a better response would be to show justice and seek justice—among ourselves: each to each, family to family, and nation to nation, knowing that is your desire. In your presence, may we—from your abundance—learn to prize a generous justice and seek it for everyone on earth.

Amen.

May 21

Kindly Presence: When life is painful

Spirit of God, kindly presence, it is only on our most
thoughtful level that we can think of you as kindly: yes, you
create our very existence, you never abandon us, you give
us freedom and accept the cost of our choices. But when
you tossed this whole cosmos into being with its unfolding
evolution in process, something greater than mere kindness
was in your heart. You dreamed of a colossal and near
unbelievable creativity, dwelling as love and outgoing charity
in human hearts. We give thanks for that despite the pain and
unpredictability that is part of it all.
Amen.

May 22

Love Is Mystery Day: When seeking understanding of love

God of All Creation, nothing more mystifies science than
altruistic love, that unselfish affection that delights in the success
and happiness of someone other than ourselves. We are made
for all of life, but especially are we made for this crowning
strength: an outgoing, other-centered love. On your divine
drawing board, surely it was a joy for you to design one earthly
animal so amazing that it could resemble in some small way
your own selfless, outgoing self. In faith and mystification, we
give thanks. Guide our steps in the paths of kindness and caring.
Amen.

May 23

Guilt Can Accumulate: When forgiving others

God of perfect understanding, guilt can accumulate like dust around the edges of the soul, created largely by a manipulative milieu calling down judgment on human conduct it disapproves of often for commercial reasons. However, we have learned from the prophets, guilt need not last. We know well, that our acts of ego-centrism and misjudgment are quickly expunged, if blameworthy, by our forgiveness of others. Give us always such mercifulness and the peace of soul that goes with it.
Amen.

May 24

New Each Day: Hoping for an eternal life

Quiet Creating Presence, everything around us—and ourselves included—are new each day, each hour, and each moment. Our body is replacing cells, the air is constantly freshening itself by the photosynthesis of whatever is green and growing, and our sun is vigorously spending out its limited energies, gradually running down. Everything is in flux. Yet our first impression is that everything around us is permanent. Only deeper realities help us see the truth: impermanence is the essence of everything—except yourself. And perhaps our souls.
Amen.

May 25

Open and Forgiving: On forgiving others and ourselves

If we are unforgiving, Holy Presence, if we cannot get our hearts to embrace a brother or sister who may have offended us, or to hold in abeyance ultimate judgment of a crime, then how can we hope to feel right about our own offenses? We are all bothered by memories of human failure and imperfection, hurtful choices that could have been more compassionate.

While you are in no way a constant judge sending us instantaneous rewards for virtue and punishment for faults, you do ask of us to cultivate a forgiving, open heart toward others. We shall do our best to achieve it beginning today. Be near, Holy Spirit, our Companion all our days. So be it.
Amen.

May 26

Praying into Silence: Sending God gratitude

To speak into the silence of your Presence, Holy Mysterious, is a privilege and a honor—especially when life is bewildering and painful. But even when life is ecstatic and inspiring, at both its extremes in fact, sending you our greetings and our gratitude is a centering and focusing act, a humanizing and grounding exercise. So at times of calm and serenity we may find ourselves turning to you as well. You are the centering fact of our life. Thanks for that.
Amen.

May 27

Full of Questions: When asking questions

Our hearts are full of questions, Mysterious God, but you must want it that way. Questions like: why are we alive? why do you not disclose yourself? how should we show gratitude for the gifts of life? why is there so much pain, so much inequality? The whole human race puzzles over the same questions, giving us an unexpected unanimity in questioning. Is that perhaps why we have so few answers? May it be so.
Amen.

May 28

With Reverence: When hopes are infinite

Holy Presence, creator and destiny of the world and the cosmos, who knows each of us perfectly, loves us for all we are and can be, who understands our hearts, with reverence we thank you for this day of life we've never lived before. We join in the symphony of consciousness and liveliness that plays out before your face. When we combine the abundance of your outpouring goodness, our limitless appetite for life, and the apparent dissatisfaction with lives all too short, we suspect more life awaits us after our earthly death. Give us enough faith to consider that possible, and enough hope to welcome whatever destiny awaits us.
Amen.

May 29

Spirit and Source of All that Is, as your spirit and your intelligence has its way each hour with all the elements of what we call evolution with the gradual unfolding of reality toward greater complexity and ever new forms of life, so may your spirit and intelligence have its way with us. May your desires prosper, God of All, in our own small part of creation, both with our bodies and with our minds as they contribute to our communal life, and with our hearts as they learn to cooperate with and surrender to what is coming about, what is evolving, in this creation.
Amen.

May 30

In the temple of your loving presence, Holy Mystery, we seek tranquility. Life is gracious—that is our faith as well as our discovery—though evil and disappointment are profoundly troubling. Our spiritual aim is to be at peace with life and death, to forgive anyone who may have done us an injury, and to believe we are forgiven for injuries we may have done. Creating Spirit beneath all that is, on balance, we are richly blessed. We give thanks.
Amen.

May 31

Friendly Presence, our God, when we are in despair, we can
turn to you in faith, and know at least the goodness of being
alive, the value of our existence, holding on to the hope that
we can be useful somehow to this world. In the darkness, we
reach out and know that you are there, and you who give
being to us also give us a purpose, something to accomplish
despite all appearances that make life ambiguous also. Grant
us vision enough to see our purposes today.
Amen.

JUNE

June 1

Vision Is Crucial: When seeking perspective

What a perspective you must have, Holy Intelligence, Infinite
Mind, knowing each of us on this vast planet with all our
human powers and limitations. Your vision of the human
scene includes both what is admirable and what is sad, our
longing for honesty but our penchant for illusion. Things
around us appear real, yet the essence of everything seems to
be its very impermanence. Change is continuous. Life is real,
but death is real as well. We turn to you for inspiration to carry
on amid this mystery. Be there.
Amen.

June 2

Working With Nature: When feeling a part of life

We praise you, Holy Mystery, for the joy of hope. Our hearts
reach out in trust for all those we love, for all our fellow
humans, for animals and atmosphere and clean water and
fertile soil. We hope the blossoming of the cosmos and of
our planet and its life continues, that we will each blossom
gradually into our full selves, our destiny. Thank you for hope
and for its joy, and its call to us each to help it all happen: the
fulfillment everywhere of all the capacities of the human race.
Amen.

June 3

Youthful Energies Remain: Giving thanks for God's plan

The world of things alive and growing surrounds us, God of Life, and we feel renewed. Our life pulses along with the blazing sun, the sweeping winds, the vigor of new births, new buds, and the caring of human parenting and affection. Human love enlivens our hearts as it does all over the earth, thanks to our astonishing powers of communication and relationship. We give you thanks, Creating Spirit, for contemplative energies that are born in us, that often stay with us our whole lives.
Amen.

June 4

Zero and Emptiness: When searching for God

The emptiness of colossal space, of endless time, of the human spirit in a search beyond the visible, Holy Mystery, defines the parameters of our spiritual journey. They are without limit. Still we shall not discover you whole among physical things or in history or in scientific research. You are darkness, otherness, and absence transformed by faith into presence, love, and light. When we leap headlong into the void, there you are, your incomprehensible self available to us and the humble words of the human mind. May it be so.
Amen.

June 5

Into Your Silence: Being grateful for evolution

God of this creation, of this day, of this moment in life, we speak words into your silence—but with profound reverence. Our heads are spinning with astonishment at the universe which we find ourselves in, living our lives within the phenomenon of evolution, an unfolding, changing, unfinished reality. To be part of it is an honor. We give you thanks as we look into the abyss of your endless inventiveness and energies. Amen.

June 6

Your Reality: When acknowledging God's mystery

Holy Elusive Spirit of God, your reality is worshipped in every religion—pursued, sought after, often even given a particular name, and a personality: harsh, loving, capricious, all-powerful, or unheeding. Yet our spiritual impulse never reaches its goal—for you are always an otherness beyond our comprehension. Still, in the quiet of sacred spaces, in the wordless ecstasy of blessed human moments, in the mystification of grief and fear, we seem to achieve a sense of your presence. For this we give you thanks, united with all the world in patient acceptance of things as they are and probably must be. Amen.

June 7

God of Energy: Giving thanks despite the world's darkness

God of Energy and Promise, God of this moment and of
the future, we give thanks to have hope, hope that in your
generosity you have provided for all our tomorrows though
human leaders fail in wisdom and moral courage. Illness is
part of our world as well and death is unavoidable, but hearts
of faith are not deterred by that. Though we find ourselves
suffering the pain of a still-blossoming evolution, we trust
in your abiding wisdom and love. In your presence we give
thanks for an indescribably gracious and promising world.
Amen.

June 8

Beloved Are You: Giving full thanks to God

Beloved are you, God of all creation. ultimate mother and
father, sister and brother, holy lover of humans all over the
earth and throughout history, and into all the future. Beloved
are you. You give us our selfhood, make sense of our chaotic
lives, and greet us at death, giving meaning at last to all that
has befallen. We bless you for the life and enlightenment we
have had, and give you heartfelt thanksgiving. Because you
cared for us, dreamed us up and caused us to be, we exist. We
give you thanks for all that is.
Amen.

June 9

To Be Fully Human: Praying in community

When we turn to you, Creator Spirit, we want to turn away
from arrogance and illusion, the arrogance of trusting our own
precipitous, solitary moral judgment, and the illusion and
foolishness that an isolated ego can be truly wise, separated
from the communal wisdom in the human circle. The
indispensable matrix of enlightenment is always community.
To be fully human is to live alert to all the circumstances
of human life, in a community of openness, reverence, and
compassion. Only together do we see things as they are,
meaningful but mystery-laden, part of a creation gigantic and
awesome but full of promise.
Amen.

June 10

We Would Harmonize: When needing the community

Quiet Presence at the heart of life, from whom we come,
to whom we go—we would harmonize with your creative
energies. You demand no burnt sacrifices or long rituals
and prayers. Instead you let us discover the enlightenment
of gathering in human circles of thought and action, and
of together finding a way of life that is just, communal and
compassionate. May our hearts be always open to the value of
others and the wisdom of a life together.
Amen.

June 11

We Welcome You: Harmonizing with God's way

Silent Mystery, in and around us, behind us in all we have been through, ahead of us in our hopes, knowing us so much better than we know ourselves, understanding so well the trajectory of our talents and shortcomings, we welcome you into our hearts and our work. We long to harmonize our energies with yours, asking only the intelligence to work wisely, the good sense to enjoy it, and the heart to carry on to the end. May your way prevail in the world and your wonderful purposes succeed everywhere.

Amen.

June 12

We Have No Choice: When thinking of death

Admittedly death is an awesome thought, Holy Mysterious Creator, but it has been the path of many a dear one, and of all in human history. It is part of being human, and we have no choice but to accept it—though we draw back in instinctual dread. Of course you also understand our fear of death, that trepidation of stepping into the unknown, silent world of human dissolution and total change. God of life and death, be with us at our last moment, and beyond.

Amen.

June 13

Our Full Identity: Listening for our name

Have you a name for each of us, Mysterious Creator, a word
that fully expresses what we are and who we are to you? Have
you not the creativity to name us completely, with a personal
identification that takes in all we have been, all we were meant
to be, all we still can be? Our earthly personal name says so
little—nothing, really—about who we are. We are listening for
the call of our true name, hoping that someday in the silence
of your presence we will each hear our full self called, known,
and identified at last.

Amen.

June 14

It Is a Comfort: Believing in God's care

It is a comfort and a relief, Holy Presence, to realize that you
know us in all our imperfection and foolishness. Do you
perhaps know us also as beautiful and admirable, each of
us a unique pleasure to your eyes and a joy to your heart?
Are you even delighted in our wayward words of prayer, so
often childish and deluded? Hidden God, we give you thanks
for your love, and especially for your compassionate and
caring presence here in the evolving world you created so
thoughtfully, and love so prodigiously.

Amen.

June 15

It Is Our Dream: Trusting in God's care

Mysterious God, in the face of human failure in high places, we would have hearts generous enough to be both just in anger and merciful of heart. Can your forgiving rain—that falls on just and unjust, and your whirlwind of understanding and compassion, create for us all a new earth—and a new heaven as well, where all the children of this evolving world of life and consciousness will thrive forever? It is our dream. May it be so.
Amen.

June 16

Light Breaks Through: When we are in pain

What is there to comfort us, Holy Presence, when our hearts long for a better life than the one we have? When we feel impoverished and blind, or hungry and lost, or surrounded by grotesque threats and terrible pain? There is comfort in community, when we gather together and balance our solitary darkness with communal light. In children—and in lovers— we often find joy and innocent hopefulness. Thanks for every instant when your holy light breaks through the dark clouds in our life.
Amen.

June 17

God of Light: Complaining to God

Why are you not more a God of justice, Holy Mystery, our Creator? Why do you stand by and let the lucky banquet sumptuously while the poor scramble for crumbs? How can you endure the sight of evil, of children abused again and again, of mental illness invading family life, and human spirits being attacked and laid waste? Why are you constantly not available to change things, to help? We trust you have reasons. God of light, God of mystery, we surrender to your mysterious ways: be near. Give us faith.

Amen.

June 18

The Work of Your Hands: Asking God to explain

Unnamable Presence, our rock in uncertainty and refuge in despair, this created world spinning through space continues to be a cathedral of wonders, of astounding natural laws somehow holding their subjects to formulas and systems that have remained the same over billions of years. How can it be so? What explains that predictability—if it not be the work of an infinite mind and caring, the work of your hands? We bless you, Holy God, for your prodigious creativity, honored to be a part of it.

Amen.

June 19

Mercy Is Your Name: When hunting for mercy

Holy God, when we are in despair over human foolishness and failure, when we are perhaps even their victim in some way, you gift us with prophetic voices counseling hesitation to condemn, prudence in withholding judgment, slowness to punish or blame. If we are adamantly unforgiving, how can we ourselves deserve forgiveness in your eyes—for we are all imperfect? Is mercy not your name? Are you not, as our prophets have taught, a wise and compassionate parent? Children of yours should be the same. May it be so.
Amen.

June 20

Wonderfully Made: Giving praise to the creator

You have made us wonderfully, Holy Creator. Conceived in human love, carried in a protective womb, born in awesome pain and labor, rising as a species gradually through natural selection to language and thought and imagination, fed on earth's prodigious nurturance, and parented into selfhood—the human path is remarkably designed. Failures happen, yet wisdom can cope and on balance our species flourishes. May it be so forever.
Amen.

June 21

The Gracious Abounds: Wondering about eternal life

So very much of this world you give us, Creating Spirit, is
benign, beautiful, lovely, full of promise and productive of joy.
Disappointment and pain are part of the mix, but the gracious
and the joyful much more abound. Then why are we still
restless? Are we made for greater things, for some fulfillment
beyond what this existence can offer? The hearts you have
given us, Holy God, contain that dream and your gifts are
always a blessing, whether their meaning be symbolic or real.
Amen.

June 22

A Blossoming Universe: With evolutionary expectations

Creating Mystery, now that evolution is a part of our
perspective, we realize that we live within a blossoming
reality, an astonishing universe, part of a fertile space-traveling
planet where denizens like ourselves are expected to accept
the randomness and chance that, with divine permission
and purpose, have brought about the freedom-filled world
we love. We would live worthily and insightfully. Grace us
with wisdom and insight enough to be alert and appreciative
citizens of this evolving miracle. May it be so.
Amen.

June 23

We Bless You: When blessing God

Creator of Beauty and Life, asking of your creature-companions only that we harmonize with all that is, our instinct is to bless you, but how? Perhaps the way infants bless you, filling the future with promise. Fresh snow blesses you also, decorating your world with brilliance and refreshment, so we bless you with our prayer and our gratitude. You are the source of all we are and shall be. We give thanks with all our hearts.
Amen.

June 24

We Rejoice Now: When rejoicing in God

Mysterious Spirit God, knowing us utterly, our childish human flaws and our unrealistic bravado, we rejoice now in your blessing, in your forgiveness for our small-mindedness and your reverence for all our desires, however wayward. We give thanks that nothing can put us beyond your compassion, nor can any achievement of ours deserve the abundant love you have for us. Blessed are you, loving, forgiving, empowering Creator.
Amen.

June 25

Transforming Love: Having faith in God's caringness

Holy Transforming Love at the heart of life, we are sustained
by your presence—in us and among us. We believe in it, and
are moved by it toward becoming our best selves: searchers for
wisdom and activists for justice and compassion. Your love,
nameless and elusive, inspires us, and gives us joy despite
fatigue and failure. We shall—for your sake—witness to our
faith in you, strengthened by your ever-sustaining presence.
Amen.

June 26

We Believe In Justice: Leaving judgment to God

Give us compassionate hearts, God of Love, so we can be
forgiving. Give us hearts of flesh so we can have sympathy
with human weakness even when the cost is high and revenge
feels called for. We do believe in justice, but full wisdom is
yours alone, O God, and limited knowledge makes us humble
and hesitant to judge. Yours alone is true judgment. We leave
it to you, knowing it is in good hands.
Amen.

June 27

The Face of Human Evil: Accepting the evils around us

Creator Spirit, could anything be more mysterious than
the dark corners of the human psyche? Only your own
overwhelming mysteriousness matches it and surpasses it.
Your Mystery also emboldens us to have hope in the face of
human evil, crime and violence. Holy God of Love—who has
filled every human heart with desires, most of them good,
but some of them twisted and misguided: be with us as we
confront the dark mystery of evil, relying on the power of your
presence to comfort our fears and promise us ultimate justice
and fulfillment of our dreams.
Amen.

June 28

Chosen to Exist: Giving thanks for God's love

God of All Creation, when our hearts are cold as stone and our
minds numb, still we know our prayer is heard, the prayer
that is our past, our present and our hopes. Our very life prays,
communicates, connecting to you. The faithful sun, seemingly
still, moves steadily from east to west (that illusion which cloaks
our earth-encircling motion). Everything living cries out to
that sun for vitalization. Similarly we all look to you, Creating
Intelligence, in dependency and gratitude. We are alive, chosen
to exist today, and we give thanks.
Amen.

June 29

We Learn to Surrender: Surrendering to God's world

Unthinkable God, unable to disengage your infinite compassion for us, nor to answer every prayer we may utter, be our companion on our human journey, especially when we find ourselves unable to help a loved one in need or powerless to improve a tragic course of events. We must learn to surrender to larger forces than our own, purposes beyond our comprehension. May all be well, though tragedy unfold and goodness seem defeated. This is still your world, Unthinkable God.

Amen.

June 30

Into the Silence: Believing the world is God's own

Somewhere in every prayer we utter, Holy Creator, is the plain truth of death—our own certain, inevitable death and ending. We speak our prayers now into the silence—knowing that someday we shall also go into, enter into, that silence. You, God of All, are the silence, of course. But you are also the harmony of symphonies, the roar of vibrant oceans, the crackling of every energy-swept universe. We live in a cloud of unknowing, but we know it is yours.

Amen.

JULY

July 1

Confused at Times: When needing God's presence

Holy Mystery, you are the creator of human love and desire,
allurement and temptation—in the throes of which we can
be most prodigiously foolish. Who of us does not stand
confused at times by desire in the eyes and warning in the
mind? All this is transparent to you, all-present Spirit. Love is
your invention, the magnetism that energizes the human race
toward procreation, creativity, community, and contemplation.
We would be wise with your own wisdom. May it be so.
Amen.

July 2

We Know the Answer: Feeling special gratitude to God

How could anyone capture in words, Gracious Creator, our
proper appreciation for sheer existence? When scientists ask—
without answering—"Why does the universe bother to exist?"
the hearts of believers fill with gratitude. They know that we
know the answer. The only possible one is—because of your
outreaching goodness, your extravagant generosity, Holy God
of gratuitous miracles. We give thanks each day that you share
yourself with us.
Amen.

July 3

Far Beyond Our Words: Naming toward God

Spirit-Sophia, Invisible Wisdom, Silent Mystery, Holy
Mysterious: as we "name toward" you so awkwardly, calling
you by titles we find in ancient myths and gifted poets and
prophets, your essence remains far beyond our words and
even our imagination—but not our instinctual faith. We
rejoice in your existence and in your companionship, in your
nourishing light and your quickening presence, and give
thanks you have brought us into this promising moment of life
and being.
Amen.

July 4

Tragedy Surrounds Us: Turning to God in dark times

Holy God, if we know you through your creatures, and
perceive your elusive face beneath the essential goodness
of this cosmos, then we can take heart, for you are a God of
Love. Tragedy surrounds us at times, and human foolishness
devastating the efforts of ingenuity and heroism. Yet we search
for discernment lest we respond to human folly with our own
foolish self-righteousness, thinking it is wisdom. Be with us on
this perilous journey into and unto life.
Amen.

July 5

Everything Alive Awakens: Looking to God in the morning

We greet you, God of the Cosmos, as Motherland Earth tips
toward the sun, and the light and energy of a new day pours
in around us. Everything alive awakens from the healing of
sleep, and a new and generous day begins. We bless you for
our life, for our heart's beat, for our mind's alertness, and for
our body's every function. May all the human family find
nourishment for today's journey, healing for illness, and peace
of soul.
Amen.

July 6

We Are Caught: Giving gratitude to God for the day

God of Mystery, we are caught by forces far beyond our
comprehension, surrounded by potential illusions, filled at
times with well founded fear. Our only hope of living wisely
is within a human circle where we can share in the intelligence
of many and feel our own story is heard and accepted.
Thank you for friends, thank you for community, thank you
especially for human love, and thank you for creating here
enough of everything essential for an enlightened life. May it
be so.
Amen.

July 7

On Their Side: When wanting to be better

All-Compassionate Spirit, we would likewise be compassionate with the offenders among us. While provident in safeguarding ourselves against them, on the side of forgiveness is our awareness of our common moral frailty, and the imperative to withhold judgment. The human temptation is to clownish self-righteousness, on the one hand, and quick self indulgence on the other. We know that no one is beyond redemption: not the gravest sinner, not even the most pompous judge who is sometimes ourselves. Thanks be to you for what compassion we have, and gift us with more.
Amen.

July 8

Immediate Listener: Feeling close to God

Are you the "deity" some refer to, God of Mystery? "Deity" carries the feeling of distance, remoteness, and the theoretical. But we know you better as an intimate and immediate listener and compassionate companion. Even your face is not very far out of range: perhaps only as far as death, and at which moment we may be greeted by you in the revelation of an ultimate reality we have dreamed of all our days. Be there, Divine Liveliness that energizes the universe! Energize us for each day, for life, for love, for wisdom, and especially for gratitude.
Amen.

July 9

Invisible Presence: Blessing God with all our heart

Invisible Presence, accompanying each of us along our journey
up the mountain of time, through the valley of the shadow of
death, under the ambiguous sky: we bless you from afar, as it
were. We know your force stretches to inconceivable distances
in every direction. Yet everything close—by also has its being
from your hands. We welcome your presence at the heart of
our lives as well and in everything we do. You are our God.
We belong to you. We give thanks.
Amen.

July 10

The Tragic Milieu: When hoping for the best

The world we know, the earthen scene, Creator Spirit, is
abounding in trouble: hungry families, abused women and
children, unjustly imprisoned men, hoarded resources,
stockpiled weapons, and an exhausted environment. Without
exaggeration, the human milieu is, in many perspectives,
tragic, even catastrophic: but not hopeless. Yet each day
children are born, young minds search, fresh hands take up
leadership dreaming of making things better, love has its way.
The mystery of your inexhaustible creativity gives us hope.
May all your divine dreams come true.
Amen.

July 11

Your Generous Being: When wanting to live generously

Loving God of life and death, creator of love, your caring
touches us and gives us hope. Give us the spirit of your caring
heart. Even when anger and violence abound in our world,
your presence and promise do more abound. We thank you for
pouring out your generous being, for choosing us for existence
and a too-short life in this challenging and awesome universe.
We would have that same generosity in responding to the
needy around us. May it be so.
Amen.

July 12

The Shame We Feel: When feeling limited

Is there some way, Spirit Creator, we can better deal with the
shame we feel over our personal limitations? Can you give us
heart? In your eyes, we are loved, certainly, as we are. There
is beauty and strength in our minds, there is goodness in our
souls—perhaps enough to face any day with confidence, if we
are wise. Perhaps if we are forgiving of others, we shall feel
forgiven for being no more than ourselves. Grace us with that
thought. Perhaps there is room for our imperfect life, in the
exact world we have, for those who do not always succeed,
even for ourselves. May it be so.
Amen.

July 13

Words Desert Us: Depending on the divine energies

When words desert us, God of Silence, when we feel utterly
poured out and bereft of energy, we rest in you: in the thought
of you and in the community of you. We often say you are
"one God" but can we really think of a singleness in the
Ground of all that is, in infinite energy? Instead we rest in
the mystery of you, in your unapproachable light, and your
unquenchable inward fire, dwelling in us all.

Amen.

July 14

Thankful To Be Inheritors: Depending on history

God of All Generations, when we think of times past, of lives
past, or wars past, of human victories and human defeats
past, the dramas in human life, the wonders of all creation,
the poetry of human achievement in science and creativity,
we give thanks to be the inheritors of the faith, the courage
and wisdom accumulated by our beloved forebears, men and
women who have passed their promise and their histories to
us. May we live our temporary lives wisely, thankful to have
the illumination others have provided for us.

Amen.

July 15

True Human Love: Giving thanks for love

Self-Giving Mystery, ultimately unimaginable by us, do not
our hearts expand when we encounter true human love, two
people thrilled with each other, lost in joy, drawn to each other
like matching magnets? Such love, capable of inspiring heroic
achievements, is perhaps your greatest gift, woven into human
fabric as earth's most intimate reflection of your own essence.
We value it among creation's greatest marvels, and give thanks
for all its wonder.
Amen.

July 16

Peering Through Shadows: Enjoying the light of mystery

We do not really know you, Holy God, but find ourselves
always peering through shadows, not perceiving anything
with clarity. The elegant universe around us and our restless
hearts whisper of your mystery, but our philosophical efforts
are seldom illuminative. You are often darkness to the mind—
but the very daylight itself to the heart. Because you exist and
entrust us also with existence, life has meaning, and joy, and
hope. We give thanks.
Amen.

July 17

Absurdly Unknowable: Prayers deeper than words

Holy Presence, once our sense of the sacred becomes deeper than words, once our need for communication with you becomes irrepressible, we use more and more prayers that are nonsensical, nothing but groans and sighs. The words need not make sense at all—for the inspiration is often beyond sensible words, addressing you, a god absurdly unknowable but still every heart's desire. Be there—where we are—in hope and in faith.

Amen.

July 18

Mystery Within Mystery: Being grateful for faith

Holy Mystery at the heart of creation, giving all that is its very existence, we sense your presence in this lively world, with every sprout that buds, with every young sparrow that soars, in every seeker of meaning in the vast human circle. Life bursts outward as well as inward, and opens an abyss of complexity almost beyond belief. Are you not the mystery within every mystery? Holy One, we are alert to your beautiful song within everything that is. It is a delight to our ears.

Amen.

July 19

We Simply Give Thanks: Prayer for spiritedness

God of mystery and unimaginable inventiveness, who has
created each of us in all our beauty and multifaceted energies,
we give thanks this day for what we are and for what we
have, for our own mysterious life forces and for our hopes
for more of this life tomorrow. We simply give thanks to be
and to be ourselves and to be linked to those we love. Give us
courage for the unique life journey that is ours, and give us
spiritedness to live it joyfully.
Amen.

July 20

Never Adequate Gratitude: When fostering great desires

Holy Creative Mystery, our God, the words of humans cannot
begin to utter adequate gratitude just for being alive, and for
being here at the end of an almost infinite chain of cosmic,
evolutionary events that produced ourselves. We not only are
alive, but we can see, we can think and remember, and know
love. We give thanks. Words fail but desires succeed: for that is
all you can ask of us.
Amen.

July 21

Unforgiving Ways: When asking for a generous heart

Forgive us, gracious, all-knowing God, for our unforgiving
ways. We easily forget our own need for forgiveness, and
indulge in the illusion of personal innocence. More real is the
insight that we are all imperfect, and our unforgiving ways
are proof of it. You are a God of mercy, mercy for each of
us, including those we are inclined to blame. Take us a step
toward innocence, and give us forgiving hearts.
Amen.

July 22

When Humans Fail: When angry with injustice

God, may we be merciful when humans around us fail. When
we witness political injustices that set our blood boiling, let us
still practice mercy—like your own. As to the perpetrator, your
judgment is true as the turning stars, as firm as the mountains,
as deep as the sea. Justice prevails and shall prevail. As for
ourselves, while we stand forever against human evil, we do
not, can not, assess it. That role is yours. Give us the wisdom
to know both the passion for what is right, and the mysticism
of mercy. We need both.
Amen.

July 23

In Your Hands: Feeling close to God

Standing in the midst of mystery, my God, I feel very much a child, with only a child's perception of my surroundings, and almost no defenses against whatever dangers may await me: the unknown threats to my life and well-being, enemy hearts that may turn against me, or the terrifying need to find my way home. You are my father, O Infinite strength, O Limitless generosity, as well as my mother, and an encircling love. Your energies are on my side, I have absolutely no doubt—because of who you are to me, and I give deep thanks this is true and that I know it.
Amen.

July 24

To Be More Creative: Thrilled to be alive

Holy Mind and Awesome Energy behind the magnificent phenomenon of evolution, we give thanks for our own minds and forces with their drive toward creativity, rejoicing in our existence and our functioning. We would be ever more creative in expanding our caringness to include the good of our entire human community along with harmony with all other life and with our precious earth habitat. May our hearts embrace the goals of your divine desires, and enjoy the thrill of being a part of something spectacular.
Amen.

July 25

The wonders of your creation, Holy Creating Mystery, give us hints of who you are. When we notice in humans our astonishing connectivity—how families and friends can remain quilted together for long years, and despite the passage of time, still find caringness fresh within themselves—then we see what a powerful, loving entity you, our Source, must be, for you have created every kind of love that we know. You are the very inventor of tenderness, of desire, of affection, and of admiration. We shall reverence you all our lives, Mysterious Creator.
Amen.

July 26

You Seem To Reply: Learning to be at peace

Should we be concerned, Loving Creator, that we may not fully use our talents, that we have not yet discovered our truest calling? You seem to reply (from outside of time) that peace of soul is our God-given vocation, that almost infinite potential remains in us—simply because you are God and you love us, enigmatic as that love must be. We can set aside anxiety. Instinct gives us hope all shall be well. May it be so.
Amen.

July 27

My Inmost Self: When learning to pray

Our simple prayers to you, words like these, God of Mystery, are not lines in a play or words in a poetic song. They are more the sigh groaning in the earth's wind or like the cry of southward-bound geese in autumn: natural, part of earth, inevitable. What reaches out to you, Unknown Creating Spirit, is who we really are, not humans taking a role to be acted out, or a melody composed by somebody else. It is our own soul's drama, the music of our inmost self. It is our truest heart choosing to speak into your silence. May it be a joy to you and a comfort to us.
Amen.

July 28

What Matters Most: Praying despite doubts

Invisible God of mystery and contradiction, what should we make of the fact that many of our fellow humans deny your existence, or find the "God question" uninteresting or of little value? About half the entire academic community, tens of thousands of highly educated people, call themselves atheistic. But in a way are they not just as faith-filled as we—for, unable to prove your non-existence, they must take a leap in the dark also, and hold their view without certitude? What matters most and unites us all is reverence for each other and for our awesome world we have been given lodgings in awhile. May it be so.
Amen.

July 29

What Does It Matter: When thinking of death

What does it matter, Holy God, how we look at and think of death—just as long as we find comfort in our thoughts? We may speculate, converse, meditate, pray, or grieve-in-advance. There is not very much we need to know about it, obviously— or you would have provided it to us all. We do know death comes to all living things, and that it shall come someday to each of us. Our traditions have provided comfort: some say that at death we are going home, back to the mystery we came from, that we are in good hands in the meantime, that all shall be well. May it be so.

Amen.

July 30

How do We Appear?: When feeling God's joy

How do we humans appear before your eyes, Holy God? As one family, spread haphazardly all over the planet, speaking to each other in hundreds of evolving languages, finding pleasurable nourishment for ourselves each day and cultivating food sources for tomorrow, enjoying the rituals of human relationship, fun, conversation, love-making, study, rest, and healing? Are we beloved to you? Fascinating? Promising? Pitiable? Or are we, with all our faults, the joy of your heart? May that be so.

Amen.

July 31

Call It Atheism: Accepting the faith of all

We give thanks, Gracious, Loving Presence, for the spiritual relationship that we share with all of humankind wherever they are found. Even instinctual doubt, skepticism, and disbelief and we may even call it atheism—brings humans together if it does not arrogate truth just to itself, if it honors the human circle and values the experience of all, even when someone's personal faith is unconventional. We are grateful, Holy God, for the very diversity of our faith journeys and for your unpredictable part of it. Guide our hearts.
Amen.

AUGUST

August 1

Limitless Future: Considering eternal life

Holy God, you observe us transparently and love us as you have made us—with all our flaws and all our promise—plain for you to see. Because you admire the work of your hands, we rejoice in our strengths and our selfhood, fragile as it may be. Because you fill us with promise—in our energies, in our intelligence, in our relationships—we rejoice in hope and look forward to tomorrow. May we turn our flaws into occasions of creativity, looking forward to perhaps a limitless future, another name for yourself. May it be so.

Amen.

August 2

Not Someone We Can Name: Unable to name the ultimate

Mystery Universe Spirit, our God, invisible energy and wisdom beneath and within all creation, have you a name? Shall we call you Sophia, or Lord, or Creator? All of these seem inadequate. You are not really something (or someone) we can name—except in analogy or metaphor, moving from things we understand to you yourself, whom we don't understand. Unnamable Entity, our God, loving force, Infinite Future, we greet you in the silence, in the cloud, in the darkness. Be with us.

Amen.

August 3

Children of Your Womb: When learning about pain

You never abandon us, Mothering Creator; for that we give
thanks. You share our pain each minute, each day. All our
life long, we remain the children of your womb, and we
are in your heart forever, even when the winds of chance
and randomness trouble us to the core. Especially in the
threatening darkness of our mortality and that of those
we love, we put our faith in you. Your way is best. Is it not
essentially an honor to share with you in the pain and life of
the world? May it be so.
Amen.

August 4

We Have Our Doubts: When learning hope

Ocean of Mystery, your unknown depths of vitality, energy,
and creativity, your presence here, is awesome. We each have
our sorrows and doubts, our personal unknowns—but we rest
in you, our spiritual habitat, so different from us. Ultimately
we will be at peace however, for while the fabric of our own
human life is impermanence, we feel swept toward a destiny
that is stable, firm, definite—and toward knowledge that is
eternal and satisfying. We would believe in you, Holy God.
Help thou our unbelief.
Amen.

August 5

Comfort In Instinct: Reaching for God's mystery

There is comfort, beloved God, in the instincts of humankind
over all the ages: that you are with us, a caring Spirit. We are
not wandering about in absurdity and chance, in a world
essentially hopeless. There is hope, and it is you. There is hope
also in human intelligence, the paths of mind that discern a
benevolent habitat here and can find meaning beneath life and
death. There is hope in every human heart—where created
love and passion speak hesitantly of a God—our Creator and
our home. May it be so.
Amen.

August 6

So Much Pain: Reaching for meaning

Are we not pitiable, this human—merely human—race, lost
and adrift in the infinite cosmos: save us, Compassionate
Presence, if you can. So much pain, so much bewilderment:
why? So many human lives that fail, that fall victim to
delusory convictions and unworthy dreams. Is there a
rationale for the evil in it, in pain, illusion and failure? From
some high perspective, is there meaning in creation's wildest
malfunctions? It is our hope that there is, that sometime in the
future we shall understand evil better. May it be so.
Amen.

August 7

Our Poetry of Choice: Searching for words of prayer

We are at a loss, Holy Spirit of the Universe, to give you a name. Calling you "holy" is itself a gratuitous choice implying your goodness and requiring a leap of faith on our part. To use the pronoun "you" is another gratuitous choice. Some would insist on "Thou." Again and again we experience awe at the world's ambiguous contents and energies, but on balance are they positive, lightsome, benevolent? We easily think of you as present, but are you a personal being, an unambiguous "you"? It's our poetry of choice—for now. Receive it as our best effort, and hear our prayer.
Amen.

August 8

Remembering Departed Ones: Looking toward death

Holy God, considering our personal death somewhere ahead on the calendar, we think of your presence with comfort. Remembering our departed loved ones is comforting as well, for they, on balance, though also reluctant to die, were rich and successful after all. They finished the race, their long journey is over and done. In the end, thankfulness is their prayer and ours, mystified by the anxieties of death—but anchored in an instinctual faith and hope.
Amen.

August 9

That's a Prayer: When finding prayer ambiguous

God of Promise, we know that prayer cannot be totally in vain.
When needy children turn to us, we grant them first a hearing,
then genuine concern, then a loving response of some kind,
though not always able to grant their particular desire. So we
know our own prayers to you are heard however childish they
may be. We feel moved to hope you are there, then to faith that
it's true. That's what matters most. In our very greatest needs,
however, we may say nothing: we just throw up our hands!
But that's a prayer, too. May it win your benevolent approval
and loving response.
Amen.

August 10

Mystery Everywhere: Discovering the divine on all sides

We thank you, Spirit-Presence of Earth and Sky, for our life,
that we are alive and functioning among so many astonishing
other creatures. In the vitality of wild things, we sense your
own unapproachable life, finding traces of an awesome
and unnamable mystery everywhere in the world. Is it not
yourself, Holy God, alive within all that is, making it to be
and to be itself with all its astonishing reality? We give you
thanks for the gifts of your majestic creation around us. We are
honored to perceive your creating vitality within all that is.
Amen.

August 11

Mystery Beyond Reach: Being touched by an eternal desire

Holy Mystery beyond our reach, we do pray for guidance
through the conundrums of life, in hope that our
disappointments serve you somehow, or serve somehow
to empower forward the world's benevolent trajectory. For
if impermanence—as the Buddhists say—is the essence
of everything, that is not only frightening but somewhat
comforting too. For while we must continually say goodbye
to those we love and cherish, shall we not eventually say
goodbye to pain also, and to sorrow, and to tears, and perhaps
to impermanence itself? May it be so.
Amen.

August 12

This Desert-Wandering Tribe: Joining with other believers

Living Creator of all that is vital, our human life is a mix of ups
and downs, bright colors and drab ones, light and darkness. I
unite my prayer today to that of all believers and half-believers
in the world, knowing that as they look for you in mosques,
temples, pagodas, synagogues, and churches—and in the sacred
spaces of nature and selfhood—you are there. And here—in this
place and at this moment. I give thanks for my own existence,
and my membership in this desert-wandering human tribe,
heading—we fondly hope—for the Promised Land. May it be so.
Amen.

August 13

Your Presence Everywhere: Greeting the Divine Mystery Gracious

Living God, we sense your presence everywhere. You are more
intimate to me, it is said, than I am to myself, for even when
I may be not self-aware—in sleep, for instance—you know
me totally and care for me. You are a living God, alive as we
are but infinitely more vivacious and vital, alive with caring,
with intelligence, with creativity, and we know not what plans
for our future. Create in us a living awareness of you, despite
your surrounding cloud of mystery and your unthinkable
energies and infinite intelligence.
Amen.

August 14

We Feel Ashamed: Judging as God's judges

We feel ashamed before you, Generous Spirit, when we are
ungenerous in our judgments of others—but is this not simply
our intellect searching instinctively for causes, for explanations,
for meaning? What matters is our second question: is our
judgment true, is it accurate, matching the divine and fully
accurate view? If we live in your presence, then your judgment
of things becomes part of our question, and a non-judgmental
wisdom is possible for us, trumping our instincts. Dear God, be
with us throughout our journey into and out of life, and make us
truly wise, forgiving, and as generous as yourself.
Amen.

August 15

You Cannot Hum To Us: Praying with confidence

What do we do, God of All, when days become ugly, when the pain or the disappointment in life becomes excruciating. You cannot take our hand or hold us close, hum us a comforting tune or tell us a pacifying story. But you can be there in other ways, be there in the person of friends and family, be there in our memories of better times, and in our hopes that good times will come again. And they will, they always will: that is our faith. Pain is part of it all, but just an impermanent part.

May it be so.

Amen.

August 16

We Glimpse at Night: Praying with awe for all creation

Spirit Presence, God beyond all that is, we glimpse your awesomeness at night as the cosmos glimmers around us. Beauty almost indescribable shines in the crescent moon. Planets glow like unreachable fruit on the swirling vine of solar magnetism, while sparkling stars and galaxies tell of an almost unthinkable reality far out of reach, at distances beyond thought.

Still within it all, we hear your very heart. Distances and unthinkable speeds only emphasize the wonder of your being and caring. We give thanks to know of your existence, and, by faith and love, to feel intimately in your presence.

Amen.

August 17

The Mystery of Love: Finding God in love

Among the greatest mysteries of life, Holy Creator, is that of
gender, of sexuality, and of love and instinct. Living things
are often found divided into sexes, and this great division not
only baffles us, but pleases us too—as sexual magnetism does
its work, creates its joy, and reproduces the on-going miracle
of life itself, or at least the desire and love for life. Is not all
this drama and heated ecstasy somehow your own primary
self-revelation, especially when love spills over, goes beyond
gender, and strong attraction trumps convention? We give
thanks for love, and its ever-unfolding mystery.
Amen.

August 18

To The Holy Temple: Praying without guilt

We never need to live with guilt very long, Holy God of
Caring. To the holy temple of your presence we possibly bring
regret, possibly inadequacy or grief, but never the poison of
perpetual guilt—for you are infinitely forgiving, prophetic
leaders say. They add: "Forgive others: and you are forgiven."
Your divine heart is that of a wise and indulgent parent, a
heart where love dominates all and understanding washes
us clean of failure, where our hopes can be as infinite as we
can imagine, and guilt as far away as east is from west. May it
always be so.
Amen.

August 19

Your Constant Care: When yearning for faith

Father of my heart, holy presence beyond image and metaphor
but inspiring them, have you gathered up my childish tears
and inventions, have you in your cosmic memory added up my
reluctant heroics and heartbreaks to prepare for me a reward at
the end which we hope is also a beginning? Spirit beyond our
knowing, we feel your being in us, ahead of us and even above us
in everything, and your joy in our never-ending outreach to you.
As you give us being, give us faith, not more than is wise but not
less than the wise hold dear. You give us your very name, Holy
Being; also give us the joy of your face, however obscure it is now.
Amen.

August 20

Our Search Continues: When reaching for God

Our mystic search continues this day, God of All, our robust
journey into love and knowledge, our joy in those we love,
our attempts to live up to our challenges. Still, we are made,
designed, to rest in you—but taking everything in human life
with us: the love, the toil, the failures. You are our heart's home
and our soul's destiny. Such rest is natural just as death too is
natural. And death is also rest, our sojourn on earth over at last.
Accompany us, Holy Mystery, each new step of the road, and
guide our way. At times we feel unsure, and far from home. Your
presence is everything to us.
Amen.

August 21

Spirit Beyond Imagining: Bewildered by the ultimate

Unimaginable Spirit, we must think of you as living in time,
yet you don't. We must imagine you able to hear our words;
instead you merely hear our hearts and our very being. We
may at times ask you to help us, to save us, to be with us.
Instead of answering, you await our responses to life and
our responsibility, loving our efforts, asking our patience,
surrender and faith. Holy Spirit beyond imagining, we accept
you however you are disguised, however unexpectedly you
deal with us. Teach us to pray, to speak into your silence, with
eyes open regardless of your blinding wonders and our dark
bewilderment.
Amen.

August 22

I Take Comfort: Giving thanks to God

Invisible Spirit, I take comfort in looking back over my years
of life and realizing that my serious ups and downs have not
destroyed me nor totally discouraged me. I wonder if it is not
your interior support that made my inner survival possible.
If so, what a marvel would be your work of inspiration when
we reflect that you are intimate to every single member of
the human race, six billion of us. As part of that enormous,
grateful, mystified throng, I give thanks for life, for creativity,
for love, even for death.
Amen.

August 23

Opportunity Beckons: When full of energy

We thank you, God, for inspiration. We hear an anonymous prophet: "God made the sea, we make the ship. God made the wind, we make the sail. God made the calm, we make the oars." At every stage of life opportunity for cooperation with you beckons. We surrender to life as it is, and hope to always have the energy and imagination to add our work to yours, to identify your greatest desires for the world and harmonize with them. When life is finally over, no doubt we shall rejoice not only in your gifts of time and love and energy, but also in our work. May it be so.

Amen.

August 24

A Battered Joy: When we need mercy

When we have done wrong, God of Mercy, when guilt for moral failure burdens us, some good comes of it. Our own hearts are often moved at such times to merciful work for others—so that we can thus deserve mercy and forgiveness ourselves. No one in your world, Holy God, is beyond forgiveness, least of all our imperfect selves. We will regret forever perhaps our egotistical choices and clownish, foolish acts. Still we feel accepted in camaraderie by this merely human race, a genuine, if battered, joy. We can give thanks for that.

Amen.

August 25

Words Fail Us: When baffled by life

When soul-wrenching bad news surrounds us, astonishing
wonders continue as well: our very life, our powers of thought
and vision, our joy in those we love, the colossal cosmos
around us. Creating Spirit, words fail us in attempting to
respond to life, to be patient, to be grateful, to be reverent
enough. Hear the simple prayer of our being, neither eloquent
nor adequate, but trusting and instinctive: you are our God.
Though there is true evil, it cannot be your invention or choice.
Amen.

August 26

We Accept the Logic: When feeling hopeful

Everlasting God, we accept the logic of our state. For each day
of life, we give you lively work. For each experience of being
loved, we send our own hearts out in loving compassion for
others. For each broken dream, we look toward to your next
inventive surprise. At each day's rest, we surrender to the
ending of energies, even, in symbol, to death itself. You are the
God of it all, its ecstasy and its logic. In faith, we accept your
ways, grateful to exist, to be alive, and to live with the hope of
possessing someday a life without end.
Amen.

August 27

Thanks for Wonder: When feeling wonder

Holy Mystery behind this complex world, and somehow in
it, all that exists constitutes a baffling message from you to
our intelligence and our sensitivities. We are in awe when we
measure the mammoth leaps in time during the formation
of our cosmos and our earth, or just witness the awesome
possibilities of the human mind, its ability to create beauty, or
comprehend the dimensions of good health and of illness, or
invent elemental cures for healing. We give thanks for wonder
as we face this awesome reality.
Amen.

August 28

In Times of Distress: In times of challenge

In our times of greatest stress and distress, Holy Presence—
when much is asked of us and we wonder if we will measure
up to the challenge, when we see so clearly our fallibility,
our human limitations, our ego brimming over, our capacity
for violence waiting to be unleashed—we rejoice in your
reasonable presence. We can always turn to you. We only are
required to do what is possible. The rest is in good hands. May
it be so.
Amen.

August 29

Take My Silence: Happy in the human circle

Take my silence, Quiet Mystery, as my feeble prayer today, my mere reaching out, my dull salutation. You exist—in your loving relatedness—on all sides. It is you we encounter in all the day's opportunities, our discoveries of what the past has meant and what the future holds. It is you in your relational liveliness that makes me also relational, and able to live usefully in the human circle. There, in partnership with your mystery, I know I am safest and most creative. May it be so.
Amen.

August 30

What Kind of God: When feeling bewildered

What kind of God are you, Holy Mystery, our creator? What kind of life is this one we have, when it seems to have come about by chance, and after billions of years of chaotic randomness? We are baffled. Do we matter? Where are you? Why do you take so little pains to make your presence known on earth, especially when that presence is almost the only atmosphere in which we can insist that justice, not chaos, rule human affairs? We are bewildered. Be with us.
Amen.

August 31

Everything in Flux: Searching for enlightenment

Amazing Creator, everything around us—and ourselves
included—is in motion, is changing, is renewed each day,
each hour and each moment, and we are grateful. Our body
is replacing cells daily, photosynthesis replenishes the air
around us, and a warm sun gives heat and radiation to all
living things. Everything's in constant flux. Yet our initial
impression, our prevailing illusion, is of permanence. We
would be wiser. Enlighten us however you can.

Amen.

SEPTEMBER

September 1

You Are Good: Knowing God is good

You are a God of Love, Holy Mystery within and around us,
for your creation is crowned with the lovingness of fertile
earth and warming sun, of insect and flower, of workers and
elders—of lovers and of children. We give thanks to be alive
and we open our hearts to an ever wider circle. Just as nothing
physical on earth is ever destroyed, only changed, so may
we have confidence that, despite our impressions of loss and
hopelessness in death, even that is somehow good: our world
is good, and we ourselves are good, and you are good.
Amen.

September 2

Dusk Into Dawn: Accepting diverse religions

Compassionate Creator, we find the beliefs of various religions
as different as day and night. For one religion, you are present
only in special places, you hear only the prayers of authorized
people; for others, you are capricious as a dance, to others
unimportant, or totally unknowable. Perhaps we shall know
more in the future—when this earthly darkness of mind turns
into dawn. Meanwhile our hearts go out to you, Holy Source
of love and energy, our God of Mystery.
Amen.

September 3

A Revelation: Being alert for God's guidance

Keep us alert to your fields of force, Holy Creative God. Is not
the migration pattern of the monarch butterfly a revelation of
an almost other-worldly engineering design? The astonishing
air-mobile insect, scientists say, can follow the earth's magnetic
field because magnetite in the butterfly's tissues detects
direction. Guide us also, Holy Creator, in whatever way you
can. No less than butterflies, we need your help along the
journey of life, to stay alert and responsive to all your fields of
force.
Amen.

September 4

Life Is Precious: Staying alert to life

God of Everything, if life is precious, our green earth is
precious and every part of it. Should we not thank you
continuously for the air surrounding our planet? Should we
not thank you for the fertile soil we plow up and cultivate, for
the rain storms that sweep across it and enliven it, for every
single burgeoning seed and bud and leaf, for every human
energy dedicated to the work of making life possible? We also
thank you for our own greatest liveliness: our limitless human
yearning for love which may be the very force of evolution.
We give thanks to you now and always.
Amen.

September 5

Where To Find You: Seeking God's heart

We often find emptiness when we attempt to reach you,
Mystery Spirit, when in human foolishness we try to make
you visible, audible, and touchable. We often find comfort
in an inspired book for it creates a kind of permanent place
where we can go to find you. A shrine or historic location
also may give us a sense of the awesome, a holiness of place,
speaking of great things past. But it is your own heart we seek
most, Holy God, your loving presence. All else is unsatisfying.
Guide us.
Amen.

September 6

A Friendly Universe: Accepting life as it is

Holy God, we choose to believe that our universe is ultimately
friendly, that all the unknowns and randomness, and all the
evils and dangers that surround us, are still the work of your
hands and heart, and that ultimately all shall be well. The
forces of genuine freedom do prevail, but the result of freedom
shall in the end be benevolent: that is our belief. We give
thanks for having that spirit of faith, and are determined to
live in its light. May it be so.
Amen.

September 7

The Sight of Warfare: In time of war

God of Life, how do you endure the sight of warfare, or the massacre of innocents? How do you deal with the delusional convictions of egotistical leaders and their armies that wreak havoc on civilizations, bringing death to hopeful humans by the thousands and the tens of thousands? We join you in your sorrow, in your despair. For respite, shall we reach out today to our own loved ones? Perhaps your love does the same.

May it be so.

Amen.

September 8

We Pray On: When praying badly

Holy Mystery, this world's creator, humans believe in prayer even though they can't explain how it works. Usually it doesn't "work" in fact, but they continue their belief partly because they can't but believe you must be benevolent and powerful, and eager to help. But you have limited your power partly to the numinous forces of evolution and partly to human choices. Still we pray on, often nonsensically. We cannot do otherwise. Be with us, Companioning Spirit, in our mysterious unknowing.

Amen.

September 9

Where Is The Past: Praying with faith

Where is the past, Enlivening God? Where is the ocean of life we have traveled across and the lands of memory we have left behind? Can life be meaningful if nothing of its heroism and challenge, its excitement, its fun and creativity, remains, if the past is utterly lost? Since you are the miracle-source of our life and of all that is, to somehow archive all that has been should be no impossibility for you. Our hopes are infinite. May our faith and our dreams come true someday, at last.

Amen.

September 10

Creator of Miracles: Hoping against hope

Creator of Miracles, of harmony in contrasts, of symmetry in chaos and rainbows amid hurricane-like devastation, can you indeed bring good out of evil? Out of pain and failure, terrible violence and defeat, can you bring hope, even success? This is your world. We will trust you are somehow within it and beyond it, calling it to completion, despite all tragedies. May it be so. We refuse to despair.

Amen.

September 11

With Awe: Expanding our vision

Holy Creator, Mothering Spirit, we acknowledge your presence with awe and gratitude. We have our creative work just as you do, our mental work, our compassionate work, our solving of life's puzzles and decisions, our openness to others. Heart to heart with you, we stretch our concerns to those we love, to those who need us and whom we need. Our prayer— to ourselves as well as to you—yearns for a widening circle, an ever larger love. May it come to pass.
Amen.

September 12

If You Exist: Giving God trust

If you exist in some sense, Holy Mystery, God of Life, then it is you we go to at death. And it must also be you we came from—for evolution and vitality can only be—ultimately— your own force empowering life into being and change. Along the way, you companion us as well, something we are aware of all too seldom. Be our inspiration, then, our comfort and our companion today, God of our life, and for all the rest of our existence. We entrust ourselves into your hands.
Amen.

September 13

To Face Death: Reverencing the depths of life

Holy God of Life, though we have to face death all our days,
it is clearly not death but life that we were made for. Sparrows
splash into fresh puddles even in icy December. A young
man waves, and his sweetheart stops her Subaru in traffic,
rolling down the window, shouting his name. A loving life is
our magnet and our focus, and an ending to life doesn't seem
possible. Is death a great illusion? Enlighten us about this
enigma, Holy One, if you can.
Amen.

September 14

Guide Us: Seeking to serve

It is hard for us to know what is right, Mysterious God,
deliberately so invisible to us, deliberately elusive and evasive
when our mind tries to comprehend you or hear your voice.
And it is especially hard for us to act out our persuasions
against ordinary human convention, against tradition, even
perhaps against civil law—in pursuing our sovereign way, and
in making daily choices. You see how we want to be just, and
generous, and compassionate. Guide us into prudent paths,
holy guiding Light.
Amen.

September 15

You Are Love: Knowing God's love

Holy Mystery and Ground of all being, our God, our Creator, what are we to make of love in the world? You are Love—say our most inspired writers, employing poetic language. But love, the mutual magnetism in living hearts, seems profligate, irrational, disorderly, eluding our comprehension. From morning to night we are energized by love, but never can master it utterly. Be with us today, God of Love.
Amen.

September 16

The Harsh Edges of Life: Opening your heart

Teach us, guiding Spirit, to accept the harsh edges of life as they are, without assuming to ourselves a superiority of purpose and perspective, and setting up our camp isolated on some high moral ground. Together our race has to live and converse, eat and drink, labor, love, and rest. Compassion on earth is as important as the air we breathe, and no companion soul given us by you may be left behind. May it be so.
Amen.

September 17

At Every Death: Hoping for eternal life

At every death, Holy God, there is a fund of gratitude in our
hearts for all those minutes when a beloved one enriched our
own days, and for the privilege of celebrating a finale with the
circle of believers—who believed in this life when it was alive,
and who have hope beyond this death, that it may be itself
temporary. You certainly grace us with a love energy that goes
beyond this life. For that we give you thanks and praise your
infinitely resourceful mystery.

Amen.

September 18

Days of Silence: Persevering through trouble

Some days are days of silence, God of Mystery, when prayers
won't come, when we are unable to find any words to address
to you with. But you are not silent on such days, speaking to
us in the physical language of creation, and in our experiences
of love and wonder, in the challenges of our work. We give
thanks then in the quiet places of our hearts, where faith is our
only illumination and perseverance our only hope.

Amen.

September 19

You Call Us: Feeling God's deep music

Into the full human circle you call us, Great Spirit, you call us
all, all the myriad beings that compose this throbbing, pulsing
earth. The music seems infinite, the rhythm everywhere.
Gather us in. Our aim is to harmonize with your sacred
melodies, to rhyme somehow with you, Holy Word, to dance
to your beat, rhythm maker of earth and sky. This symphony
is your creative desire. May your will be done.
Amen.

September 20

O Infinite Music: Feeling the music of life

Into the full human circle call us, O Infinite Music, to where
the unfamiliar becomes commonplace and exciting, and we
finally see how unique each human person is. As long as I
know only my similarity to my fellow choristers, I remain deaf
to the surprising concord that only difference can provide. It is
diversity that makes harmony possible, the sound of the real
as it is: not a unison, certainly not a drone only, but rainbow of
sounds. May it be so for us all.
Amen.

September 21

Wonderful God: Entrusting ourselves to God

Wonderful God, are we not in loving hands? We are. Immense
and magnetic as our universe is, ancient as are its beginnings,
complex as are its immeasurable parts, yet our hearts' longings
are still more immense, magnetized toward the mystery that
is you. They find your unknowable essence and energy, Holy
One, steadily attractive. In prayerful times we may simply let
ourselves go: toward You, into your mystery, trusting that an
astonishing order and caring lies beneath all this universe's
baffling mysteries.
Amen.

September 22

Many an Unhallowed Cause: Thankfulness for life's wonders

God of All, the religions that attempt to honor you are
numerous and diverse, some wise, some misguided. In
addition, your holy name is invoked in many an unhallowed
cause: we renounce these abuses. But we do call on you still—
as do most religions—as the source of our life, the home of our
hearts, and the object of our continuing gratitude and awe.
That is a wide-ranging spirituality worthy of our race. May it
honor you everywhere.
Amen.

September 23

God Beyond Chance: Thanking God always

God beyond chance, if pure chaos reigns (as some would say), then why is there not chaos in the way oxygen reacts with hydrogen, or chaos in the intricacies of animal and insect behavior? Whence is our predictable gravity, whence vision, whence healing energies? The likelihood is that your hands are everywhere, guiding the orderly ways within creation that prevail through time and across the entire cosmos. Guide our minds as we give thanks, as we reverence all you do.
Amen.

September 24

I Speak, I Sing: Discovering purpose in prayer

I speak to you, Holy Mystery of Life, I sing to you, not out of fear, not out of obligation, not hoping you will change my life for the better, but praying only to be a small part of the symphony of existence and of livingness that rises from everything in creation. What I speak is simple, reverent, thankful, and plain: just the earthen poetry that is myself and my heart. Hear my "prayer," as it were, my heart's beat, the throbbing vibrations of my organs and cells, the sighs of my desires. They depend on you for their energy and purposes. Be with me.
Amen.

September 25

Into My Consciousness: Praying to serve God

Come, Holy Spirit, creating me anew at each rolling moment, creative force holding everyone in existence along with all that is, come into my consciousness, speak to me in the real events of this day, and in the happenings of this entire era everywhere on earth. I am listening. I want to be a part of what's going on, to lower the level of pain and failure on earth, to add to the joy and enlightenment of my circle of friends, of my neighborhood, of my environment. Inspire me today with wise daydreams and outgoing feelings: "Make me an instrument of your peace" as your St. Francis put it so unforgettably. Amen.

September 26

A Glimpse of Beauty: Gaining strength for hard times

God of beauty and of desire, I thank you for those moments of my life in which—through living embodied persons I love—I have caught a momentary reflection of goodness itself, and an enrapturing attractiveness at its most powerful. Knowing there is such a deep level of sweetness and satisfaction in human life helps me face the shadows, the pain, and the heartbreak that life contains. I am grateful for all life's wonders, and am fortified by them for the encounter with their opposites. Amen.

September 27

Nothing to Say: Hunting for God's presence

Holy God, I have almost nothing to say in reaching toward
your elusive reality this day. No expression seems adequate,
no feeling responsive or grateful enough. I have metaphors for
you: a good mother, a caring friend, a strong father, a sky full
of wonder, a hurricane not in our control—but you are there
beyond it all, an energy, a mind, I really do not know. What
you ask of me in my life, my Creator, I surrender to, I am open
to. Your presence is my only respite place in the silent desert of
unknowing. Be with me.
Amen.

September 28

God Beyond Being: Feeling faith despite the unknowns

God beyond being—in the words of the mystic Meister
Eckhart: I know we have few words to describe you, and few
names that cast anything but clouds of mystery about you.
Still we turn to you each day with surrender and reverence,
believing we are all beloved by you and entrusted with
a mysterious and meaningful life, however absurd and
frustrating it may seem in the short run. May we live out
that belief with courage and patience, building an ever more
beautiful world and wider human circle as we go.
Amen.

September 29

Child of Your Creative Force: Accepting the Ultimate as it is found

Friendly Spirit who created me, who knows my every breath
and move, who has placed me where I am to live amidst
mystery and bewilderment and surrounded by the wonders
of nature and of consciousness, I rejoice to be the child of your
creative force. I trust I am safe within your caring—though
battered by chance and danger like all my race. You are known
to us—but only within a cloud of unknowing: never with
clarity or comprehension. We give you our faith, an option you
suggest to all intelligent creatures. Help thou our unbelief.
Amen.

September 30

You Know Me: Trying to know God

My God of Mystery, though you know me perfectly, my name
and all I am, I know you almost not at all, certainly not your
name. One theologian calls you "the relational liveliness that
energizes the universe." Relational you must be: caring for me
and all your creatures. With your "liveliness" you enliven all
that is alive. You energize everything—and all of it is packed
with energy. And the entire universe is your magnificent
handiwork. We worship you in trust and surrender.
Amen.

OCTOBER

October 1

I Cannot Not Believe: Feeling grateful to be alive

Holy Enigma, my God, mystery I cannot not believe in, from your hands I accept my life, my vitality and liveliness, my bodily-ness and my personhood. Whatever I say of you is limited by my merely human experience, but I do see you are not finite as your creations are but exist beyond us, a personal being but unnamable "other." Accept our stammering prayers and messages and hear our hearts: they surrender in acceptance and awe, grateful beyond measure to be part of your reality.
Amen.

October 2

Mindful of Where I Am: Feeling God's caring view of us

Mindful of where I am in my life, I raise my voice to speak to you, Holy Mystery beneath and within all things. Where I am may not be distinctly known to me, of course: because, like all my race, I do not really comprehend my final destination or how much longer I shall be on this particular road. But I do know where I am in relation to you: I am in your view, I am in your care, I am part of your empowered and magnificent universe. That is where I am. You would have me succeed, certainly, in finding the place I was born to find: living a life as full and as outgoing as I can make it. May it be so.
Amen.

October 3

I Speak In Darkness: Speaking to the unknown

Deity Mysterious God to whom I speak in the darkness
of faith, knowing almost nothing about your being, I put
instinctual confidence in my own mind and out-reaching
heart. It is my own complex humanity that tells me most
clearly that you must exist, and must care for us all. That
complexity, my own nature, is awesomely constructed, as are
all the parts of the world around me. For my very existence
my heart is grateful today not grateful to chance, or to a
process, or to the totally unknown ultimacy—to you, my God
and my All.
Amen.

October 4

Divine Unknown Creator: Prayer in self-absorption

Divine Unknown Spirit Creator, could anything be more
dissonant than my impulsive egotism in the face of your
gracious generosity? My self-absorption clashes ludicrously
with the rich beneficence of your outpouring hand. I will turn
my attention toward this day's gratuitousness, toward the
larger reality, with the hope of harmonizing my heart's song
with the bountiful and unselfconscious symphony of all that
is. It is an honor to be alive and aware of your surrounding
and pervasive love.
Amen.

October 5

Into the Confusion: Participation in God's dreams

Holy God of unreachable depth and height, my hope in
every crisis, I rejoice in your accompaniment of me into
the confusion of human effort amid necessarily limited
possibilities. With your companionship I shall do my best to
play my role in the drama of the days ahead, lost in wonder
over the confusing complexities of your world but confident I
am equipped to contribute to a better human outcome, to the
happiness of others and to the healing of wounds. Be with me
in everything.
Amen.

October 6

Within Me: Joining with God's plans

Higher Power, above me in some ways and within me in
every way, and below me too, ground of my being: with your
inspiration and support I feel I can accomplish today what I
must. I can be myself. I can stay linked to those I love. I can
reach out to those in need. I can bear up under whatever
burdens I'm given and can enjoy today's pleasures gratefully. I
give thanks for my life, mysterious and ambiguous as it is, and
link my desires to your own.
Amen.

October 7

You Are With Me: Cooperating with divine purposes

Can you discern the words in my heart before I say them, incomprehensible God of Wisdom and Creativity? The words are thankfulness for one more day, and the desire to be useful in some way today. You are with me, holy Presence, and I entrust myself to you once more. Whatever may come, I will not be alone. That thought is comforting, and the reality behind it almost too good to be true. Be in me with your own splendid plans, Holy Creator, and I shall in turn try to draw you into mine.
Amen.

October 8

You See My Face: Entrusting yourself to God

I imagine I am before you, my God, as I would be before an impressive human acquaintance, a parent, or a friend. You see my face, you care for my pain, you rejoice in my promise. You speak to me in the wonder of all that is, and in real events around me. It is an honor to be here in this way, and I carry on my life in your presence, something quite different from utter solitude. You are always at my side and on my side, my God, my creator, and my destiny. I give you my faith and my surrender.
Amen.

October 9

I Trust You: Trusting in the reality of God

Holy Spirit beneath and within everything that is, my own soul and substance is in your hands as are my bones and my breath. Do with me what you will: I trust you, and entrust to you all that I am and shall be. You are a caring presence: that is my faith—even against appearances. Be with me this day, enlightening my mind however you can, strengthening my resolve to be faithful to my sovereign selfhood, come what may. You are my God. I am in your hands.
Amen.

October 10

Behold Me Here: Being in touch with God

My God, my Spirit Creator, my home and destiny, observe me here in your presence, totally overwhelmed by your being and your incomprehensibility. Of course you do not require my prayers or my meditations—your care for me transcends all the superficial communications between us. We are essentially bonded in the being you give me moment by moment, and the purposes you have destined me for and draw me to. I greet you—as I will at my once-only death. You are my God, and I am your child and companion, today and forever.
Amen.

October 11

Be In My Adventures: Calling upon God

Mystery Everywhere, in every physical location throughout the universe but also in every mental space, in every human heart, in every dilemma, doubt or apparently absurd set of events or dangers, but also present in every aromatic organism propagating its fragrance, every bubbling cell in every living thing, and in every created substance following the laws of its functioning, holy everywhere-God: be in my adventures as their center, their goal and their meaning. You are everything to me—though I realize it all too seldom.

Amen.

October 12

God of Love: Prayer of searching

Holy Mysterious, could anything be more natural than to be good to those I love? Because love is your most awesome creation, some name you a God of Love. But you are the God of Everything: of life, of life's ending, of each soaring mind and each encompassing feeling and instinct, of all that's green and alive and promulgating and looking around with caring eyes, a God of planets and galaxies full of magnetism, including love. You are our God. Holy Mystery: be with us as we navigate through this cosmos of love and uncertainty.

Amen.

October 13

This Game of Faith: Prayer of finding a hidden God

From this ambiguous outpost along the coastline of mystery,
I bless you today, unknown God, my surreptitious ally, in all
your enormous reality unconvincingly pretending not to exist.
You are cloaked over in the apparent randomness and seeming
absurdity of human existence, but in the unmistakable beauty
and elegant fabric of things your fingerprints are discovered.
We have found you in the darkness once and for all, and bless
you in this game of faith.

Amen.

October 14

I Will Live Today: Thinking of death

I will live today as a flower half-opening, as a song in its
middle, not its end. Flowers know they have a destiny and
bloom that always arrives; singers know their song will
inevitably modulate to an end. Our death may be a surprise,
but not an unexpected one—yet something we need be in no
hurry to experience: it is on its way this very minute. Time is
passing on my journey to you, and I want to live with that fact
in view: human life is temporary. You, Home, are eternal. And
I am on my way.

Amen.

October 15

I Am Not Alone: Not feeling alone

You are an intimate to my heart, Caring Spirit, so you see my thoughts, my ambitions and my pain. Having your personal understanding means a lot to me: I am not alone. I give thanks. I want to be aware on this day of your presence, alert to the sacred in each of the directions I turn, and bounteous like yourself in my giving and my forgiving. My instinct is to guard myself too much: I am determined instead to be more creative and trusting. In your company I shall have a day of light and surrender, with, hopefully, grateful rest at day's end. Amen.

October 16

God Alive In Everything: Finding God trustworthy

Immortal Mystery, Holy God alive in my mind, alive in everything around me and behind me in the past and ahead of me in the future, I give you worship. You are my supreme creator, my true God. You make the sun to rise and the loving hearts around me to beat. I give thanks that you are there, as well as here, in my life today though incomprehensible. May your reign come about, your dream for this earth come true, through the wonders of human heroism and intelligence, and the upward evolution of all promising life energies. So be it. Amen.

October 17

Elusive Creator: Searching for God in creation

Elusive Spirit, Invisible Creator of this visible world, we
have reached toward you using different names, finding
some whisper of your goodness incarnated in famous people
like Moses or Jesus of Nazareth, or a touch of your mystery
preserved in the Christian Scripture or in a scroll of the Torah
or Koran. I am comforted to think that your loving self is
necessarily present wherever there exists anything you have
created. So you are here, Holy One, and everything around us
is holy with your telltale fingerprints upon it. That is a joyful
thought.
Amen.

October 18

May I Contribute Creatively: Working with God

Holy Mystery beyond our minds but not beyond our hearts,
we trust we are safely within your caring view. This is your
world, not the way you would have it in every detail, but the
way it must be to fulfill your divine dream. Today, let me be a
positive part of that dream. You would have me surrender, of
course, to today's events: I do so. But you would also have me
contribute my creativity to yours: I long to do so, I shall try to
do so. Be with me, then, in all I do in partnership with you.
Amen.

October 19

Be My Music: Praying for inspiration

At the suggestion of the Talmud, I listen for your angel, Holy
One, saying to me: grow! grow!—the supposed angelic voice
even each blade of grass hears continuously. So in metaphor I
can know the presence of your great mystery just a little: you
speak in all that is and in all my best instincts. Voice of God, be
my daily and hourly music. I would be less fearful, less numb
to creation's whispers, less hesitant to reach out to help others
and to take part in life. Provide a guiding, encouraging voice
to me today, Holy God.
Amen.

October 20

I Am Ready: Morning prayer of hope

I am ready for the future, my God, at least at this moment. You
are with me, you stand by me and steady my resolve. Nothing
is certain: collision with an asteroid may suddenly materialize
and our whole planet shattered by the impact, today its last
day. Or our friendly sun may simply rise and set above an
uneventful scene—except for the sacraments of love and
fruitfulness that make our earth its magical self. Probably a
day lies ahead somewhere in between. Be with me, companion
Spirit, Friend, and Mystery.
Amen.

October 21

My Being Speaks: Finding joy in life

When my mind is far from concentration and my heart
unfocused, still my being speaks to you, God of life, God of
promise. There is hope for me because you are a caring creator,
and have filled our experience with caringness: links of concern
and love in my heart for those around me, and energies of
positive regard from others toward me. In such a circle we can
survive, and with evolutionary imagination at work everywhere,
we can find joy in the mysterious dance of daily life.
Amen.

October 22

Holy Voiceless Energy: Feeling Disbelief

Holy Voiceless Energy and Intelligence inhabiting all that is and
this morning as well. Like most of my ancestors, I worship you.
You are sovereign in all you do and choose not to do: I am no
judge of that. Some of my fellow humans say you should comfort
us more, should be a little more visible, even more obvious. That
way we could more easily choose the good and avoid the evils
of irreverence, misbehavior, and disbelief. Do you enjoy the
sight of irreverence (when it is compassionate) and find disbelief
acceptable at times? Do you encourage doubt? I feel you must:
many of our best and brightest are much given to it. Give me the
grace to "doubt faithfully" as well, if that is ever my vocation.
Amen.

October 23

Those Golden Streets: God's nearness

It is not mandatory that in my prayer time I feel lost and troubled, Mysterious God, but just the opposite: I am only my fullest self when I am essentially at peace. Still my peace is not your peace. Mine is always a patchwork or an accident or a surprise. Yours is a land I can only dream of, something I believe in even when it is inconceivable. Take me occasionally to the outskirts of that city, Sacred Mystery, where I may see at least the reflection in the sky of those golden streets.
Amen.

October 24

Let Me Be Lifted: Trusting in God

Vast Mystery of Energy and Intelligence, Parenting Creator holding me—in some unimaginable way—in your care, I unite my limited energies to your reality. I will let myself be lifted through our communion up into my best human self, my most persevering self, my tolerant, courageous, and relational self, my out-reaching and compassionate self, in order to cooperate with you in this explosion of creativity that is every moment's reality. With faith in you in my heart, with trust in you in my mind, great things are possible.
Amen.

October 25

Grounded in You: Turning to God

You are God, the ground of existence, of all that is called being:
its creator, and our creator. All I do, all I am, is grounded
in you. You are my foundation, the underlying entity and
mind that makes me all I am this moment. When I turn to
you to pray, it has to be for you at least a little like our own
experience of children's voices and appeals: a precious sound.
So my words do not need to be eloquent or fluent or even
rational. You love my being and my talk, however it turns out.
Amen.

October 26

May I Call it Love: Feeling God's care

One of the comforting lights glowing in the darkness of my
mind, Holy God, is the thought that you observe me and care
about me in the specificity of my singular being. "You know
when I lie down and when I rise." There is no doubt that in
your vision of earth, I live, I exist. Each minute and each hour
of each day you have me—along with all my connections to
others—in your purview, before your face. At my death it is I
who shall return to you, to your earth and to your mystery. I
give thanks for your—may I call it "love"? Yes.
Amen.

October 27

In Wordlessness: Speaking without words

In silence, in wordlessness, I turn to your kindly presence
so eloquently verbal in the vivid colors of earth and sky, in
the pulsing life of the quick squirrels that scurry among the
trees, in my own heart going out to those I love. In reply to all
this, I cease my literal and wordy prayers, realizing that all
I do—my work, my compassion, my delight in those I love,
my creativity—is a language you cannot but hear. The silence
between us is rife with communication and eloquence. We
both speak and listen, a communion. Thanks.
And Amen.

October 28

My Being Cries Out: When reaching for hope

Holy Mystery, on days when I have nothing to say to you,
I rejoice to know that the core of my being cries out—in
gratitude for existence and life, with thanks also for those I
love and who love me, and in expectation of good things to
come. Though ambiguity surrounds me, still I will wait for
the clouds to clear and for the sunshine of your presence to
become more prevalent—as it always does. Meanwhile, I will
hold the course, confident all shall be well. Every winter has
its spring. Every night its dawn. There's a message in that,
from you.
Amen.

October 29

In Your Hands: In Awe of One's Self

God of my heart, in whose hands are all the energies of
the universe, all the beauty and fragrance of wild plants
crowding the roadway with gold and purple elegance, all
the sizzling explosions of light on the surface of every star,
God of indescribable creativity, you bless me with my own
personal design, and hold in being my own sizzling heat of
one amazing human life. I am in awe of myself—but of myself
in you, of your handiwork within me, and of your passionate
desire for my eternal unfolding. I utter my quiet thanksgiving
while my heart sings:
Amen.
So be it.

October 30

I Can Do Nothing: When hope seems gone

God of all wisdom, when I can do nothing to heal or improve
a regrettable situation, comfort me with your simple presence.
I know your mind sees meaning where we may see only
absurdity. Your compassion embraces pain where we may
detect no relief or hope. Your creative imagination knows
remedies and good prospects within this creation where we
may only despair. I turn to you when hope seems gone. Into
your hands I commend my spirit.
Amen.

October 31

Finding You: When God inspires

Holy Mystery, why are you more present to me when I am
in distress than in contentment? When I happen to have no
complaints, somehow my soul becomes unfocused, and I
simply rest in the peace and serenity of mind: but this surely
can be spiritually healthy too. However, in frustration, doubt,
fear and discomfort, quickly I turn explicitly to you. With your
gift of a wider wisdom perhaps I can become more balanced,
finding you beneath all my experiences, whether pleasant or
burdensome, learning to "pray always." May it be so.
Amen.

NOVEMBER

November 1

Ready to Serve: Ready to serve God

Your servant awaits, standing here ready to serve, Holy
Mysterious: yet is it service you require today? Or is it just
life you require—and give? My lively heart will, hopefully,
beat on this day, energizing my body and my self: so that
is what I present to you, my heart. May the life of my mind
find enlightenment, and the life of my heart passion—and
compassion. And in any interims, may there be humor, and
dancing, and inspiration.
Amen.

November 2

With Faith: Searching for God

Were I to die today, to the end I shall reach with my mind into
the darkness of you, Mystery beneath my own mystery, true
ground of my own mystery, hoping—as even today I do—to
feel the comfort of your presence. For some excellent reason,
you have not made it possible for us to be "scientifically" sure
of you, or even philosophically sure: instinctively is enough,
but that is not certitude. That is faith. So with faith I reach out,
Holy God, and trust you are there.
Amen.

November 3

You Shall Be With Me: When trusting in God

In your company, God of Life and of Death, I will live this day, knowing it could be my last—but expecting to live, and work, to enjoy communication and fellowship, to suffer and sympathize, to find nourishment and then rest at day's end.

I rejoice to know that you shall be with me, and by your mysterious forces in the world shall be drawing me toward my fulfillment and destiny in you. You are the sacred Mind and Heart that designed this life for us, and I entrust myself to your mystery with all that I am.

Amen.

November 4

To Be Your Servant: When companioning with God

Today is another gift from your gracious heart, God of life itself and God of my life. My functioning body and mind, my energies of curiosity and appetite, my obligations, my relationships and links to others, all are from your hand and heart. I give you my gratitude. For my part, I would be non-judgmental with myself, with outgoing concern for others, with forgiveness, with commitment to help and to care. Let me be your servant as well as your companion in mystery this day.

Amen.

November 5

Creation Is Yours: When surrendering to God

Perfectly hidden God, designer-builder of the universe,
friendly presence within and around me, today I give you
surrender, surrender to all the chaotic circumstances of my life
and surrender to whatever is to be. This creation is yours. Your
intelligence gave it its design and its marvelous randomness,
and the power of your lovingness brought it all into being. You
are my very God, my only God, and I say "let it be" to all that
is. Your way is best.
Amen.

November 6

Blest Be You: When facing life's challenges

Mysterious Source of all that is, Ocean of Life, spirit intimate
to my heart and mind, I appear before you once again, in
awe of your incomprehensibility—and longing to pray, to
communicate with you, to befriend you one more time here in
the midst of my perilous journey through human life. I thank
you for all you have done for me and those I love, and for all
you cause to happen for us: life, love, constant challenge, and
freedom. May you be forever blest.
Amen.

November 7

Out of My Silence: When blessing God

I speak to you this day, unknown God, out of my very silence, out of my ignorance, out of my darkness. It is my bones that speak, my fragile being that speaks to your permanent Being, my whisper to the symphony of your magnificence. You are my God, I am your creature. You are the day star of my world, the womb that brought me into life. I turn to you for everything, grateful to be chosen for life. May you be blest everywhere and always—as you are blest today in this human heart.
Amen.

November 8

God of My Childhood: When not fathoming God

You are the same God, Friendly Mystery, as the God of my childhood, of my highest hopes, of my darkest hours—though now I know enough about you to hesitate to name you in any particular way, using any word that implies more information about you than I have. In my grown-up prayers, I seek to be, above all, honest with myself. Inspire me today in my life long journey into the unknown, content with the Cloud of Unknowing that is my life's habitat.
Amen.

November 9

It Is Not Honest: Knowing God's compassion

Despite all my reflection about you, Holy Creator, it is not honest to say I know your name, your gender, the look of your face, or your particular location or holy residence, or your will, for that matter. One thing I do believe must be true: that you have a heart for those in pain—because that quality seems supreme in all conscious beings as well, and may be therefore our most intimate window on who you are. All-compassionate Spirit, be our God.

Amen.

November 10

All You Are: Feeling God's Presence

All the days of my life, Holy Spirit, you've known me utterly: my risings in the morning, my daily plans, all that happened each day, and how I felt as I lay down—so many hours, so many minutes of my life. Time is your gift. I have it again today, and give you thanks. Be with me once again, Companioning Mystery, this time perhaps with more awareness and acknowledgment on my part of all you are to me. Ocean of unknowing, cloud of presence, God of my life, be near.

Amen.

November 11

I Entrust Myself: Seeking to trust God

God of supreme knowledge, surely your mind masters every contour and quality of our physical universe: from the vast cosmos with all its speed-of-light movements and forces to the last, most intimate element in cells and in molecules, atoms, electrons and quarks. Is there something you do not know? I suspect you do not know, and cannot know, the future—because it isn't yet real. Yet your guesses have to be prodigiously wise. I entrust myself to your knowledgeable caringness.
Amen.

November 12

My Prayer, My Self: When unable to trust prayer

Holy God who is real—not the all-powerful "lord" of everything or the sweet old man in the sky, but true Ultimate Mystery and Ground of Being: hear my prayer. It is your real creature's voice you hear, the soul of my soul speaking in words and beyond words. I sometimes fill a void between us with verbalizations like these: it's just a bridge to the comfort of your silent nearness. But my soul's soul knows the language of silence as well, and, behold, my prayer: my self. Nothing more.
Amen.

November 13

I Become My Best Self: To the God of Love

I thank you, Ocean of Life, for the people I love, for those who make me vigorous and give me peace. In their eyes I become my best self, and in their presence I feel all will be well despite whatever darkness threatens. Even death is—in many ways—thinkable in the circle of love, and for this I am deeply grateful.

Nothing at all stands against love. It conquers sorrow and despair, all horror and threat, all loneliness and fear. It outlasts and overpowers them all. I thank you for the love I know, your own most precious creation and gift.

Amen.

November 14

Invisible As Air: When mystified by God

O God, as present and vital to me as air and as invisible, God unknown and magnificent beyond my wildest imaginings, you are like a mother to me but endlessly more caring, like a father but warmer, stronger, like a brother or sister but more companioning, a lover and friend but even more faithful. Intelligent fashioner and lover of everything that is, I give you praise. You are everything to me: my God and my all, but almost unknown.

Amen.

November 15

You Know Me Utterly: Facing God

Facing you, as it were, Holy God, is unlike any other encounter in my life. As the ancient psalm says, you know when I sit down and when I rise. The metaphor helps. You do know me utterly—but that is a joy. It simplifies, focuses life. Before you I am my simple self, transparent and cared for. As for my faults, my faith in your mercy and understanding is more important than any amount of self reproach. Before your eyes, I am my best self, loved as I am: your good creation. Amen: May it be so.

November 16

My Problem: When called to faith

Your invisibility and silence, Spirit-Mystery, Holy God, is a problem. We do not hear you or see you: why is that? Or am I being dense? For you do speak to me in everything that exists around me, and your beauty is visible in dozens of directions: in the sunrise, in smiling faces, in the celebration everywhere of life and love, in the sparkling sky each night, and the spinning colossus of a grey-green mother earth full of life. Your silence is a problem, God of All. Yes: my problem. My lifelong problem and daily mystery.
Amen.

November 17

Give Us Guidance: Seeing the unknown

God of this creation with all its cosmic unknowns, Holy Genius
Spirit behind the enigmas of nature, and of living creatures and
above all of humankind, hear our voice today. We are in awe of
our complex ability to reason and remember and understand, and
our gift of pleasure in others and of love, sexual and altruistic.
What should we make of our inclination to speak this way, into
your silence? Does it make sense? Are you there, here, listening?
Give us guidance in our passionate questioning into what's going
on, and alertness to all the sacraments of your presence.
Amen.

November 18

Where Can I Turn?: Seeking Wisdom in the silence

Holy Mind, Ocean of Energy, infinite God, my surroundings are
humble, but my needs are great and overwhelming. Where can I
turn for wisdom, for enough intelligence to manage my choices?
It is comforting to know you are with me, God my Creator and
Companion, with awareness of my mind and my resources, and
readiness—if it energizes your own desires—to empower my
native consciousness and perspicacity. Be with me, holy Spirit, in
my meditations, even in my instincts. With your empowerment, I
can be as wise as I should be, and learn to live with failure if that,
on occasion, is my lot.
Amen.

November 19

God of My Day: My plain being prays

God of my day, Spirit Companion on whom I totally depend
for reassurance, for energies, for accompaniment through
frightening places, even for guidance if that is imaginable:
I have no lyrical prayers at this moment, no theological
fireworks or heroic achievements to draw your attention, just
my needy being. Is that enough? My being and my needs, my
apprehensions and my vulnerability? Be with me. I give you
my allegiance because I must or I will be even more at sea than
I am.
Amen.

November 20

I Hope It's Trust: Speaking into God's mystery

Holy Real God, it is just me who speaks to you today, my
plainest unvarnished self, my sometimes delusional and
egotistical self, almost ashamed to raise my voice here in
the midst of your beautiful reality and among so many
extraordinary human spirits. Many times I think: the only
thing uncommon about me is my impertinence in speaking
at all when, with all my failures upon me, I break into your
awesome silence. I hope it's a modest trust in your goodness—
not impudence—that gives me voice, however halting. May it
be so.
Amen.

November 21

Come With Me: When God is with me

Come with me, Creator Spirit, in all that happens this day.
You see my need for strength, for focus, for perseverance.
Inspire me with these if you can. Above all open my eyes to
see things whole and not superficially. Open my hearing to the
music and promise in my own heart's beat and in its flights
of affection. Guide me if you can in healing whatever wounds
I can affect. Make me a useful part of this fantastic earthen
scene, my temporary home, my essential place of work,
human linking, and becoming.
Amen.

November 22

In The Darkness: When losing faith

Creator Spirit to whom I reach out in darkness, wondering if
you are there and what difference my prayer might make: real
life is a challenge to faith. The very design of living things cries
out in praise of your intelligence and imagination. But when
our forces begin to fail, when our bodies break down, when
we become ludicrously egocentric, when heart-ache comes and
hopes are crushed, we can lose faith—even in you. Be with us
in the darkness, Holy God of light.
Amen.

November 23

I Am Not Alone: Feeling a connection to God

Speaking to you, Communicative Creator, is not a task only of my mind or even of my heart. My very existence speaks, and my relationships to others speak. My existence says I am yours. My links to others say I find you everywhere, I am not alone. So, however I may fail at faith or at prayer, I am a prayer, my whole dynamic is reaching out and finding you. We are in communion, and I am safe. I have learned to trust that ultimately all shall be well. May it be so.

Amen.

November 24

Come Holy Spirit: Trusting in the future

Come, Holy Spirit, and—if it is your way—visit my mind, the mind of someone you first dreamed up, then created and shaped within my mother's womb, then accompanied all the hours and minutes of life, and whose destiny is safe in your keeping, whatever that may be. Dear ones die and seem to leave us behind, but their path is the very same journey we are on. Perhaps we shall catch up to them. No one knows, but may our dreams come true that a greater life is always ahead.

May it be so.

Amen.

November 25

I Praise You: Admiring God's creativity

Sacred Spirit whom I know as the incomprehensible energy
holding me in existence: astonishing physical forces do
surround me, all designed by your intelligence and held in
existence by your being-giving love. Wonderful are all living
things, as are the ten thousand diverse "machines" in each cell
of a living body to convert the food we eat into usable energy
and organized matter. Infinitesimal forces vibrate deep within
us, while our cosmos expands at its outer limits. Your world
is remarkable beyond words, and, just by existing, praises
you—as do I.
Amen.

November 26

Largely Foolishness: Feeling loved by God

I speak to you, Holy God, as if you were a friend facing me,
someone I am endlessly in awe of. But such an image is largely
foolishness even though it is the best I can do. You are not "a
friend" like any other friend. You are not a human person at
all—you are spirit, not so much a being, but the very ground
of being itself and of every being, the essential liveliness from
whom all living things come, our incomprehensible creator. I
bless you though the darkness of your mystery, and reach out
to you, a privileged soul whom you love. May it be so.
Amen.

November 27

It Is Comforting: A prayer full of hope

Holy Sustaining Presence, on days when I feel uninspired, and
unable to muster up the imagination to speak to you in prayer,
it is comforting to remember that you have no such days or
hours: you love me into being each moment I exist. You are
present to my needs and aware of everything in my life, never
remote from me—as you may seem in my imagination. You
are the Mystery that holds me always, holds me in being,
holds me in selfhood, and cares for me without limitation.
May it be so.
Amen.

November 28

One More Day: Praying with confidence

Thank you, Gracious Spirit, that I have this day to be alive,
to enjoy the bright warmth of the sun, the faces of my life
companions, our planet's air to breathe, the earth's food to
enjoy. Should death come knocking at my door, or illness
arrive, or disappointment be my temporary companion, I must
endure it—but not alone, and not without hope. It makes sense
that the mysteries around us challenge us to faith, to hope, and
mostly to love given and received. This is a benevolent world,
all in all, and I am grateful.
Amen.

November 29

You Called Me: Praying with long term perspective

Holy Presence, as you called me forth in life's beginning, may you welcome me at life's end. I add my voice in thanksgiving to you for this challenging journey. Like a flower I am called into selfhood by the mothering sun of people who care about me. Nurtured in every way, I discover love and gratitude in my heart, and then over time I become a self and blossom for the benefit of all. Finally I realize this earthly experience is transient—though an inner yearning for life carries me forward in hope. Your way is best. I give thanks.
Amen.

November 30

I Speak Thanks: Giving thanks expansively

Today I give thanks for my consciousness, able to leap back years and decades to recall memorable events and people I loved, able to leap forward to delightful prospects ahead, aware of the present moment and of the fascinating things and people around me. I give thanks today for the amazing laws of nature enabling sparrows to swirl in hundreds overhead, my own heart to beat, all life around me to go on. I speak thanks into the darkness of mystery, feeling I am heard. May it be so.
Amen.

DECEMBER

December 1

Your Way Is Best: Entrusting yourself to God

When the unknowns and uncertainties become crushing to
me, I can still turn to you, Mothering Spirit, and feel your
solid ground under my feet. Even more solid than the earth
is your Eternal Being. I will rest in the darkness of faith, and
comfort my heart with acquiescence to what is. I may as well.
No amount of dissatisfaction will change my essential lot.
This is the world you would have me in, a world without
certitude, where challenges surround us, and only faith carries
us through: belief in ultimate goodness. I entrust myself to you
partly because I must. Your way is best.
Amen.

December 2

You Are Present: Praying in God's presence

I am going to imagine, Creator Spirit, that the prevailing
instincts of our human forebears have been essentially correct:
that as you are present to all the things you hold in existence,
that you know everything that is, and thus you know our minds.
For me it matters greatly: you know my mind. I need not speak
aloud therefore, or move my lips, or find some kind of holy
words to say—though all of these may help me focus. You pay
attention to my every thought—and this moment my thought is
comforting: you are here, you care, and you hear my heart. I give
thanks for that.

Amen.

December 3

We Smile at You: Praying with joy

A smile can be magical, Creator Spirit: what an invention!
We give thanks for every loving smile we've received in our
life, every facial expression of silent body-language that says
"I'm pleased with you," or "You are a joy." Faces otherwise
unremarkable, carrying all the marks of the past or anxieties
for the future, suddenly dawn with a smile at someone, and
joy and appreciation flash between two mysteries. So with us,
Holy God. We smile at you this moment, and feel you smiling
too. You are Goodness, our Source, our mother and father, our
lovers and friends, our hope. So be it.
Amen.

December 4

Eyes and Sight: When experiencing imperfection

You see me as if with millions of eyes, Creating Mystery: you
know me well. My resolve is imperfect, my courage less than
firm, my commitment weak, my compassion flagging, my
spirituality more ego than altruism. But you are accustomed
to imperfection: your purview takes in all the earth and all the
cosmos. Evolution continues: the creation is unfinished. So I
rejoice to think my unfinished self may fit right in. May it be
so.

Amen.

December 5

Behold Me Alive: When exalting in the morning

Behold me alive another day, Divine Creator, a day I had no right to expect to be given. It is a gift from your mysterious hand, from your hidden heart: and I know I am loved. Out of the darkness of your mystery I am blessed by you, and I bless you in return—as does all of creation. Blessed are you, God of earth and sky, for you have invented us magnificently, and gratuitously. Blessed are you, Loving Mystery, my creator and my God.
Amen, Alleluia!

December 6

I Turn To You: Blessing God for all that is

I do not turn to you, Loving Creator Spirit, just to cope with the frightening things along my life path—though knowing your existence is comforting at such times. I turn to you today because I believe you to be my natural home, my goal, and my meaning-giver. In a sense you are everything to me, and in a way you contain everything of importance: vitality, intelligence, and caring. In each day's darkness, your name is a word of light, but you are the fire at the heart of light as well. I bless you for those creative flames and vast energies.
Amen.

December 7

You Are My Companion: Putting faith in God

You are the companion of my most private thoughts, Holy
Spirit of Life. The chaos, the pain and the uncertainty in
my soul and mind are well known to you, and you alone
are my strength and my hope in dealing with them. Can
you enable me to be my best self today, self-forgiving of
my incompleteness and courageous in living with the wild
diversity of this creation another day? Your creative womb
gave me being, holy God; you could not but care about me. I
put my faith in you.
Amen.

December 8

I Offer Myself: When feeling inspired

Spirit, wise and caring, I offer myself to life this day, trusting
you are with me and in me. Wherever I go, whatever my task,
we shall do it together: "not I, but God in me" as the mystic,
Dag Hammarskjold, thought of it. In companionship with
you, nothing can be impossible: facing my fears, living with
limitation, doing worthy work even imperfectly, and patiently.
Nothing is beyond my energies—when joined with yours.
May it be so.
Amen.

December 9

These Natural Medicines: When feeling depressed

Compassionate and Companioning Spirit, you know well
all the personal flaws and imperfections that I sometimes
blame myself for. You understand how any mind injured
by childhood experience—by illusion, by shaming, or
manipulation—can swim at times in a sea of anguish. I offer
myself today to your healing inspirations: the awesome beauty
of tall ancient trees, the laughter of children, the touching
poetry of familiar music, the colors in the sky. Heal me with
these natural medicines flowing from your hands.
Amen.

December 10

Only My Silence: Praying without words

There are days when every thought and prayer I have for
you, listening Spirit, come to nothing. I can give you only my
silence. But perhaps that is ideal. After all, my silence answers
your silence. You address me not in words, but in happenings
and in events. You speak in the genial morning sun moving up
a golden sky. You speak in my body functioning without my
volition. You speak in those who care for me and speak to me
honestly. My appreciative response to each of these will be my
prayer to you today.
Amen.

December 11

Teach Us To Pray: Learning what prayer is

My words to you, God of All, seem to gradually dissipate
into silence. The bowing of my head, even the homage of
mindfulness, seem to have no effect or value in the real
world. Yet prophets assure me I have a most alert listener:
your Loving Self. They say when I honor your presence, the
world—all that is—moves toward what it was meant to be, a
giving and a receiving, a word and a response. Teach us then
to pray in that way: perhaps it may be what we were born for.
Amen.

December 12

Satisfied With Me: Enjoying God's call

Creator God, Infinite Future, I hear in the silence the whisper
of my true name. It came not from an infancy ritual. My
name is my very self uttered by your infinite caringness,
and promising life beyond all my imaginings. It says you
are satisfied with me, even delighted with me, full of hope
for me. Its sound sets my heart at ease, and gives my soul
wings. I an eternally grateful to be the promising person I am
in your eyes. Let your plan unfold as perfectly as it can, and
forgiveness for failure be plentiful—as it is.
Amen.

December 13

Be My Familiar: Finding God in everything

Could you become my "familiar," Holy Mystery Creator,
so I might see you everywhere, in everything? Might I see
you in the expression on my infant's face relating to me at
last? Familiar with your artistry in the quilt of darkness that
transforms the window view at night? Know you in good-
tasting red wine, in unselfconscious human beauty, in the
dread that seeps into our heart as we read of war, of earth's
fragility? Be my familiar, Holy Mystery, my God! My hope is
that you can make it happen.
Amen.

December 14

I Applaud You: Being touched by eternity

I applaud you, God of Life, when I see the sturdy gray rock
doves suddenly explode and surge up through the tree
line and out of sight. The modest bubbling inventiveness,
the creativity in my own head, is humbled by your own
profligate cosmic inventions: the rainbow, the eye lash, the
glistening lake, the work of musical genius. If this world seems
sometimes also disappointing, surely that too was meant to be.
Perhaps it all points to the future, and faith can take us there.
May it be so.
Amen.

December 15

God of My Faith: Knowing what is right to do

When I feel I must do what I should rather than just what I love doing, my heart turns me to you, God of my faith and of my conscience. There are obligations I am convinced of because they make sense—believing you have put us in this world for a purpose, in a world that also makes sense partly because we're in it. I call this an act of "faith" because I do not see or feel the rightness, but somehow know it is right nevertheless. It is right to seek justice, to love kindness, and to walk in companionship with you, Holy Spirit: though nothing could be more challenging. Be with me.

Amen.

December 16

Mysterious God: Living with doubt and faith

Beloved Presence, in one way more to me than any human friend or parent or lover, more than any person of inspiration: my admiration and awe of you is profound. You choose not to be visible, not to be easily familiar, not to give yourself even a decisive name. Mysteriously, you support in being ominous entities that threaten and attack human life, in a cosmos apparently temporary. Mysterious God, I believe, but with uncertainty. Help thou my unbelief, my disbelief, my doubts.

Amen.

December 17

Holy Universe: Praying with wonderment

Do you hear my voice, Holy Heart of the Universe? Does it
make sense for me to put words together in a prayer, to think
of myself as facing you, as addressing you, as heard by you?
If you are indeed there—here—and are necessarily a God
with total knowledge of what is, then you do know my spirit
and all the secrets of my heart and mind? Why should I speak
words if you already know me perfectly, except that I am
constantly becoming my fuller self? Send us light for that task,
friend God; make it morning in our soul.

Amen.

December 18

God of this Day: Praying with confidence

God of this day, remote from me in comprehensibility, intimate
to me in my body and mind, I give you my personal worship,
Sovereign Creator of all that is. Whatever may become of me, I
abrogate my freedom to rebel against life, to be self-absorbed,
or to choose isolation. You yourself are the force that draws us
into the future, into the unknown, and unto our destiny. We
give thanks that what happens shall make sense, and for the
life of challenge and intimacy we have.

Amen.

December 19

A Joy to Live: When blessing God

It is a joy to live in your presence, Creator Spirit, to know your caring is near, your intelligence as well, and your infinite resources. This means my ultimate fears, my serious fears, are foolish. You care about me, you know every way to protect me, and—within the limitations that go with this creation— you can save me from every threat. I have a God intimately involved in my life, and it is you. May you be ever blessed.
Amen.

December 20

Death not Unthinkable: When thinking of life's end

Death is usually an unpleasant thought, Creator God, no matter how I present it to myself. It shall probably be a challenge and an ordeal, for myself and others I love, yet you ask it of me. Life itself asks it of me. Perhaps—since it is a natural process—it need not be over-dramatized or allowed to frighten. My death is not unthinkable. What is unthinkable is to have to go through it without your presence. Be with me now and at the hour of my death. May death be the bright arrival of your unmistakable, all-fulfilling presence.
Amen.

December 21

What Your Eyes See: Seeking the strength of compassion

What your eyes see, All Compassionate God, and what mine
see differ almost infinitely. Your heart goes out—the wise
have written—as does a mother's to all the children of her
womb, warming first to the most helpless and pitiable of
them. My own eyes are dim and faulty, and my heart is often
disconnected from the marginalized and luckless. Inspire me
with mother-like compassion this day so I may be for others
an instrument of your caring.
Amen.

December 22

God As You Are: Giving thanks for prayer

Holy God as you are, not as we've inadequately pictured you
in myth and analogue, Sacred Mystery as you exist in your
incomprehensibility, hidden in your cloud of unknowing.
Nothing I say to you today will necessarily bring about
something other than what already is happening: you are not
a God we can manipulate, although your care is infinite. Still,
my words of prayer are rituals of my mind that carry me to a
place of meditation, of concentration, of focus, where I enjoy
being an undefensive self, and where I know you with a little
more clarity than at more scattered times. I give thanks for the
privilege of prayer.
Amen.

December 23

Here I Am: Praying despite ourselves

Here I am, Mystery of Presence, my God, my Meaning: you
have found me. This is prayer, the feeling of your presence.
You find me even when I do not find you, even when I am
bewildered by an avalanche of images, utterly distracted,
mentally somewhere else. So I place myself here in peace of
soul before your eyes in the presence of all my fellow humans,
one person in the vast human circle. You have found me and
taken hold of me. You are my link to everything. So be it.
Amen.

December 24

All Is Possible: Feeling known by God

Here I am, God of Life, a person you are thoroughly familiar
with. When you hear my cry, you look at me: you are by my
side. Welcome, Companioning God. Our race has often erred
in welcoming you fearfully. We have slaughtered animals,
attempting to give them as gifts to you. We have trembled
and cowered, flattered and cajoled. No more. Behold your
companioning servant, myself. In your presence, all is
possible. Guide us in our sensible worship of you—if you can.
Amen.

December 25

Welcome to My Heart: Knowing God's presence

Welcome to my heart, unbelievable Partner God. With You I
walk along life's path. You are acquainted with all my sorrows.
You know well my limitations, my jagged scars, and my
unclosed wounds; but you know also my self-transcending
vocation, my yearning for connection with others, my precious
and interdependent selfhood, my true name. Speak to me every
mile of the way, Holy Loving Life Companion. Urge me on.
Amen.

December 26

Your Ultimate Music: Confident God is present

The silence of this hour, Holy God, vibrates with your ultimate
music. In the darkness I feel the clear day of your mystery.
Your love for me is written in the wind, in the quiet, in the
mist. Ultimately, I have no fear, for nothing can separate us,
Giver of Life and Hope. I shall never be alone or left behind or
abandoned or homeless as long as you exist and I exist. You
have made me for a miraculous existence, for love, and for
yourself. May it be so.
Amen.

December 27

From You I Emerge: Joy in community

Intimate Spirit, closer to me than my skin, closer than my
eyes, closer than my thought is to my self, here you are,
Unimaginable God. From you I emerge at each split second.
Toward you I move, moment by moment. To you I inexorably
go: you are home. In the human circle I overcome my
anxieties, for together with others no one gets lost, all are
heard, and we can be wise. I will listen to the prophetic among
us, proceeding with caution but with faith in your guiding
presence. May it be so.
Amen.

December 28

I Turn to You: Believing in a God

Dynamic Friend Unseen, Mystery everywhere, in creating
this world, you made a reality where you yourself could hide
almost perfectly. The thought of you is a comfort, unknown,
unseen God. When anxiety surrounds me, when worry and
uncertainty grips me, I turn to you for respite, to your mystery,
to your hidden reality. You are meaning, you are hope, you are
future—though all unseen. In faith is comfort. May it always
be so.
Amen.

December 29

I Survey the Future: Finding joy in Others

God, my God, anxiety simmers in my soul when I survey the future. Shall I have humiliation to put up with, pain to endure, disappointment in my greatest dreams, loneliness and shame and failure? Where is there respite from such worries? Certainly it resides in those I love, in those who love me. These people satisfy my need for hope and rest, all of them paradigms of your own reliable, surrounding love. May it be so.
Amen.

~

December 30

I Am Your Child: Being a part of the world

I am your child, Holy God, simplistic as that statement sounds. I am the earth's child as well, a small part of her mysteriously thriving life, breathing her atmosphere, living from her products and offerings, a companion of her animals and living things, with ties of reverence to all her amazing continents and oceans, to the mysteries of her mammoth body beneath me and of her role as a planet-home in the cosmos for billions of fellow humans. I am honored and give thanks.
Amen.

December 31

A Long Small History: Having a sense of God's presence

Your Presence, unnamable Spirit-Force, reminds me of
journeys on earth where you accompanied me, of each
past day's beginning and end, each beloved morning and
afternoon, each descent into sleep, sweet or troubled. We have
a long, small history together, Holy God, and you are the very
God and Source of truth, of everything that has transpired in
this creation since the great explosion at the dawn of time, and
eternally before that. Be in my heart all my life, and especially
during the hours of this day, and all my hours and days will be
precious.
Amen.

Thematic Index: Prayers for Special Purposes

Prayers of Awe

January 4 ~ Finding God in the morning
March 3 ~ Amazed at God's love
March 27 ~ When searching for magic
August 16 ~ Praying with awe for all creation
August 27 ~ When feeling wonder
November 26 ~ Feeling loved by God

Prayers of Bewilderment

January 17 ~ Trying to understand God
February 10 ~ Finding God elusive
March 5 ~ Relying on God
April 2 ~ Praying amid ambiguity
August 21 ~ Bewildered by the ultimate
August 30 ~ When feeling bewildered
December 23 ~ Praying despite ourselves

Prayers at the Time of a Death

January 21 ~ Hoping beyond death
March 1 ~ When thinking of death
March 9 ~ Thinking of death
June 12 ~ When thinking of death
July 29 ~ When thinking of death
September 12 ~ Giving God trust
September 13 ~ Reverencing the depths of life
September 17 ~ Hoping for eternal life

Prayers in Times of Depression

January 22 ~ Prayer about darkness
March 10 ~ In times of pain
April 5 ~ Praying in despair and sadness

October 4 ~Prayer in self-absorption
October 30 ~When hope seems gone
November 22 ~ When losing faith
December 9 ~ When feeling depressed

Prayers in Times of Doubt

January 7 ~ Reaching out in the darkness
January 20 ~ Praying amidst darkness
July 28 ~ Praying despite doubts
August 6 ~ Reaching for meaning
September 8 ~ When praying badly
December 16 ~ Living with doubt and faith

Prayers of Forgiveness

February 9 ~ In times of failure
March 2 ~ When seeking to forgive
May 23 ~ When forgiving others
June 19 ~ When hunting for mercy
July 7 ~ When wanting to be better
July 21 ~ When asking for a generous heart
August 24 ~ When we need mercy

Prayers when a Friend is in Need

February 4 ~ When praying for others
July 25 ~ Giving thanks for love
October 15 ~Not feeling alone
November 3 ~ When trusting in God
November 6 ~ When facing life's challenges

Prayers of Hope

January 26 ~ Giving God trust
February 2 ~ Finding hope
February 7 ~ Finding a reason to hope
March 20 ~ Hoping in darkness
April 9 ~ Hoping without end
October 20 ~Morning prayer of hope
November 27 ~ A prayer full of hope

Prayers of Rejoicing

January 2 ~ In touch with God
February 24 ~ When feeling happy to exist
September 29 ~ Accepting the Ultimate
October 28 ~ When reaching for hope
December 5 ~ When exalting in the morning
December 8 ~ When feeling inspired

Prayers of Solidarity with the Poor

January 7 ~ Reaching out in the darkness
January 9 ~ When yearning for justice
April 23 ~ Praying for peace
May 20 ~ When longing for justice
June 17 ~ Complaining to God

Prayers of Surrender

January 14 ~ Knowing God awaits us
February 20 ~ Surrendering to life
February 22 ~ When hoping against hope
March 19 ~ When resting in God
June 29 ~ Surrendering to God's world
October 8 ~ Entrusting yourself to God
November 5 ~ When surrendering to God

Prayers of Thanksgiving

January 5 ~ Believing in God's graciousness
January 24 ~ Safe in God's care
March 29 ~ Our part in giving thanks
April 11 ~ The grace that abounds
August 22 ~ Giving thanks to God
September 4 ~ Staying alert to life
September 23 ~ Thanking God always

Still at work in his 80's, William Cleary is a poet, novelist, and musician. He has authored several books, including *Prayers to She Who Is*, *How the Wild Things Pray*, and *Prayers to an Evolutionary God*. He also wrote a full-length musical based on the Confucian classic fable, "Chun Hyang Song," which was later revived for the Seoul Olympics. Cleary has written articles for such publications as *Commonweal*, *National Catholic Reporter*, and *America*. He is married to Roddy O'Neil Cleary, a Unitarian minister, and is the father of two musician sons. He lives in Vermont.